ONE FLEA SPARE

Naomi Wallace

D0188370

BROADWAY PLAY PUBLISHING INC
56 E 81st St., NY NY 10028-0202
212 772-8334 fax: 212 772-8358
http://www.BroadwayPlayPubl.com

First printing: August 1997
Second printing: November 1999
Third printing: February 2003

I S B N: 0-88145-138-X

Book design: Marie Donovan
Word processing: Microsoft Word for Windows
Typographic controls: Xerox Ventura Publisher 2.0 P E
Typeface: Palatino
Copy editing: Liam Brosnahan
Printed on recycled acid-free paper and bound in the
U S A

ABOUT THE AUTHOR

Naomi Wallace is from Kentucky. Her newest play, THE TRESTLE AT POPE LICK CREEK, premiered at the 1998 Humana Festival of New Plays at the Actors Theater of Louisville and was produced in 1999 by New York Theater Workshop. ONE FLEA SPARE was commissioned and produced in October 1995 by the Bush Theatre in London. It received its American premiere at the Humana Festival and was awarded the 1996 Susan Smith Blackburn Prize, the 1996 Fellowship of Southern Writers Drama Award, the 1996 Kesselring Prize, and the 1997 Obie Award for best play. It was produced by the New York Shakespeare Festival in March 1997 and is being produced for film by the producer of *Four Weddings and a Funeral* and *Notting Hill*. BIRDY, an adaptation for the stage of William Wharton's novel, opened on the West End in London at The Comedy Theatre in March 1997, and on the West End in Athens, Greece at the same time. SLAUGHTER CITY was awarded the 1995 Mobil Prize and received its world premiere in January 1996 at the Royal Shakespeare Company. IN THE HEART OF AMERICA received its world premiere at the Bush and subsequently was produced at The Long Wharf Theater and in Dortmund, Germany. It was published in *American Theater* magazine and was awarded the 1995 Susan Smith Blackburn Prize. Her plays are published in Great Britain by Faber and Faber, and in the U S by Broadway Play Publishing Inc.

Wallace was a 1999 recipient of the prestigious MacArthur Fellowship, the grant popularly known as the genius award.

A published poet in both England and in The United States, she has also received grants from The Kentucky Foundation for Women and The Kentucky Arts Council, and a 1997 N E A grant for poetry. Her book of poetry, *To Dance A Stony Field*, was published in the United Kingdom in May 1995.

Her film *Lawn Dogs*, produced by Duncan Kenworthy, opened successfully in Great Britain, moved to the U S, and has won numerous film awards.

At present, Wallace is under commission by the Royal Shakespeare Company, The New York Shakespeare Festival Public Theater, and Actors Theater of Louisville. She has film commissions from Toledo Films and Dog Star Productions.

This play is for my children,
Nadira, Caitlin, and Tegan

ORIGINAL PRODUCTIONS

ONE FLEA SPARE was commissioned by the Bush
Theater in London, and opened there on 18 October
1995, directed by Dominic Dromgoole.

ONE FLEA SPARE received its American premiere
at the Humana Festival of New Plays at the Actors
Theater of Louisville, and was awarded the 1996 Susan
Smith Blackburn Prize, the 1996 Fellowship of Southern
Writers Drama Award, and the 1996 Kesselring Prize.

ONE FLEA SPARE was produced in New York at the
Joseph Papp Public Theater/New York Shakespeare
Festival. The cast and creative contributors were:

MORSE	Mischa Barton
BUNCE	Bill Camp
MR WILLIAM SNELGRAVE	Jon de Vries
MRS DARCY SNELGRAVE	Dianne Wiest
KABE	Paul Kandel
Director	Ron Daniels
Scenic design	Riccardo Hernandez
Costume design	Paul Tazewell
Lighting design	Scott Zielinski
Sound design	Stuart J Allyn
Original music	Michael Rasbury
Production dramaturg	Mervin P Antonio
Production stage manager	C A Clark

Oh stay, three lives in one flea spare,
Where wee almost, yea more than maryed are.
This flea is you and I, and this
Our mariage bed, and mariage temple is;
Though parents grudge, and you, w'are met,
And cloysterd in these living walls of Jet.
Though use make you apt to kill mee,
Let not to that, selfe murder added bee,
And sacrilege, three sinnes in killing three.

John Donne

Corruption is our only hope.

Bertolt Brecht

CHARACTERS

MR WILLIAM SNELGRAVE, *a wealthy, elderly man*
MRS DARCY SNELGRAVE, *an elderly woman*
BUNCE, *a sailor, in his late twenties*
MORSE, *a girl of twelve*
KABE, *a watchman and guard*

TIME

1665

PLACE

A comfortable house in Axe Yard, off King Street,
Westminster, in London.

SETTING

A room that has been stripped of all its fine furnishings,
except for a couple of simple, though fine, wooden chairs. One
small window upstage.

A cell or a room of confinement.

Street below the window of the SNELGRAVE's house.

ACT ONE

Scene One

(MORSE locked in an empty room or cell. Alone. She wears a dirty, tattered, but once fine dress. She stands center stage with the dress pulled up to hide her face. She is wearing a torn pair of boy's britches or long underwear under her dress. She is just barely visible in the dim light. She repeats the words that her interrogator might have used earlier.)

MORSE: What are you doing out of your grave? *(Beat)* What are you doing out of your grave? *(Beat)* Speak to me.

(We hear the sound of someone being slapped, but MORSE remains still and does not react.)

MORSE: Speak to me, girl, or you'll stay here til it's known.

(Another sound of a slap, harder. MORSE still does not move.)

MORSE: What happened to the Gentleman?

(Another slap)

MORSE: What happened to his wife?

(Another slap)

MORSE: Whose blood is on your sleeve? *(Beat)*

(MORSE drops her dress down to reveal her face.)

MORSE: The blood of a fish. Is on my sleeve. Because. The fish. The fish were burning in the channels. Whole schools of them on fire. And the ships sailing and their hulls plowing the dead up out of the water. And the

war had begun. The war with the Dutch had begun.
(Beat) It was March. No, it was later. In summer.
A summer so hot vegetables stewed in their crates.
The old and the sick melted like snow in the streets.
At night the rats came out in twos and threes to drink
the sweat from our faces. *(Beat)* And it had finally come.
(Beat) The Visitation. We all went to sleep one morning
and when we awoke the whole city was aglow with the
fever. Sparrows fell dead from the sky into the hands
of beggars. Dogs walked in the robes of dying men,
slipped into the beds of their dead Masters' wives.
Children were born with the beards of old men. *(Beat)*
They were locked in their own house, the two of them.
All the windows, but one, nailed shut from the outside.
They'd waited out their time of confinement. Three
more days and they could escape.

But then we came. In through the basement and across
the roofs.

One of us died. In that room. Two of us died. *(Beat)*
It was night. Yes. At night. He moved as though
invisible. Gliding through the empty streets.

*(BUNCE, making a fair amount of noise, tumbles into the cell,
which has now become the SNELGRAVES' room. He stands
facing into a corner.)*

MORSE: He came in through the cellar. He thought the
house was empty and so he made himself at home.

(SNELGRAVE and DARCY enter their bare room.)

MORSE: But his timing was off. Mr and Mrs Snelgrave
caught him in the act of relieving himself into one of
their finest vases.

*(MORSE joins the scene, but hiding in the corner. Everything
freezes. Then lights go up on BUNCE in the SNELGRAVES'
house. BUNCE is looking over his shoulder at the
SNELGRAVES, who remain in the shadows, almost invisible.)*

BUNCE: *(Producing the vase, with a genuine embarrassment)* Thought I'd. Save my piss. It's got rum in it. Might be the last I'll have for weeks.

(End Scene One)

Scene Two

(Lights up on the SNELGRAVES' *room.* MORSE *is still hiding.* SNELGRAVE *and* DARCY *jump back, terrified of contact with* BUNCE.)

BUNCE: I'm a poor man looking for shelter.

SNELGRAVE: My God! Lord have mercy on us!

BUNCE: I thought everyone died in this house.

SNELGRAVE: Help! Someone help us!

BUNCE: Shhh. I mean no harm.

DARCY: He's relieved himself. In my vase.

*(*BUNCE *holds out the vase, offering to give it back to her.)*

DARCY: Get out of our house.

SNELGRAVE: He has the infection!

BUNCE: Not I.

SNELGRAVE: He's lying. He stinks. And sick. Look at his eyes.

BUNCE: I'm not sick. Just hungry.

SNELGRAVE: The guards. What if they saw you enter?

DARCY: They have no mercy; it's the law.

SNELGRAVE: Open your shirt. Stay! Open! Prove there's no marks on you.

*(*BUNCE *opens his shirt. With his cane,* SNELGRAVE *pokes at* BUNCE, *moving the shirt this way and that to have a better look. We see a bandage around* BUNCE's *waist and a spot of blood.)*

SNELGRAVE: What? There's blood. My God! Blood!

BUNCE: It's years old.

SNELGRAVE: *(Brandishing his cane)* Get back! Get back!

BUNCE: Still bleeds.

SNELGRAVE: Your arms, then. Show us your arms!

(BUNCE pulls up his sleeves and SNELGRAVE examines his arms.)

SNELGRAVE: No other marks. He's clean.

(MORSE comes out of hiding. All three of them jump back.)

MORSE: I am Morse Braithwaite.

SNELGRAVE: There's another! God have mercy.

MORSE: Sole daughter to Nevill and Elizabeth Braithwaite.

SNELGRAVE: Back, vile trespasser!

DARCY: Sir Nevill Braithwaite and his wife. We know them.

SNELGRAVE: Dead of the plague last Tuesday. Man, wife and daughter.

MORSE: It's true my father fell on me in a fit of fever and there I lay beneath him for two nights and a day. It's terrible to smell such things from a father. But I finally dug my way from under him and up on the roofs I went. To hide. To hide from the plague. I saw no light in this house. I came in through the window. I'm not a thief.

SNELGRAVE: Open your collar. Let's see your neck.

(MORSE opens her collar.)

DARCY: Sleeves.

(MORSE pulls up her sleeves and they examine her.)

SNELGRAVE: Shame. Shame on you both. You could have infected this house.

(Banging at the window)

SNELGRAVE: Both of you. Quickly! Crawl back out of this house, whatever way you came in. Hurry. Hurry! Before you're known.

(Banging at the window again. MORSE *and* BUNCE *hide.* KABE, *the guard, peers in, thrusting half his body through the small window.)*

KABE: Good morning, Mr, Mrs Snelgrave. Have a good sleep, did you? It stinks in here, it does.

SNELGRAVE: We've washed the floors with vinegar.

KABE: And stripped the room bare, I see. Well, the less the nasty has to hide in.

SNELGRAVE: We've boarded up the other rooms, except for the kitchen.

KABE: Ah. Shame it is. Such fine rooms, some of the finest in town maybe, empty but for stink. Bit cramped this one though?

DARCY: This is the only room where someone hasn't died.

KABE: Ah yes. Two maids and a house boy, carted and pitted. And the canary too, Mrs Snelgrave?

(He makes the sound of a canary.)

KABE: Shame. *(Beat)* Will you be needing any provisions from the market this morning, Madame? Plenty of corn but cheese there's none. Butter, none. Some fruit but it's got the hairs.

DARCY: No, thank you, Kabe. That will be all.

KABE: The whole town's living on onions. You can smell it in the evenings. It's all that farting that's killed the birds.

(Sound of hammering on boards)

DARCY & SNELGRAVE: Kabe?

KABE: Sorry. Fellow across the way saw you let in a couple of guests last night.

DARCY: No. No.

SNELGRAVE: You can't do this. You can't—

DARCY: Please. Kabe. We beg you.

KABE: Can't have that. They might be carrying.

SNELGRAVE: They broke in. They were uninvited.

KABE: We're doubling up the boards.

DARCY: We are innocent.

SNELGRAVE: We have good health.

DARCY: We've held out in here alive.

SNELGRAVE: Alive, damn you, for almost four weeks! We are clean!

KABE: Sorry.

BUNCE: (*Appearing*) Then why didn't you lot try and stop us?

KABE: Not our job. We're just the guards. We make sure no one gets out. If they get in, well, that's just luck. So, twenty-eight days again for the lot of you. Just enough time to get snug. I don't mind. I like this house. Pretty as a bird, it is, heh, Darcy?

(*He tweets again.*)

DARCY: How dare you!

KABE: Does stink, though. I get paid twice as much to guard a proper house like this.
Could I have one of your gloves today, Mistress?
Won't you show us your pretty white hands?

(KABE *shrieks with laughter.*)

SNELGRAVE: I'll have you in the stocks when I'm out of here, Kabe.

KABE: I've been wanting to ask her that for years. Never could 'til now. (*To* MORSE) Why don't you ask her? Ask her to show you her pretty, white neck! (*Sings*)

One o'clock, Two o'clock, Three o'clock, Four
Here's a red cross for your door.

Where's my enemy?
Flown to the country!
Never mind that, coz'

DARCY: Someone should shoot him.

KABE: One o'clock, Two o'clock, Three o'clock, Four,
I've got the key to your locked door!

(Shrieks again with laughter and is gone)

SNELGRAVE: Come here, child.

(MORSE approaches him. SNELGRAVE slaps her.)

SNELGRAVE: You would have been better off if you'd
stayed put. Sir Braithwaite's daughter doesn't climb
over roofs. Sir Braithwaite's daughter doesn't enter
uninvited. Your father is dead. Give me your hand.
In the Snelgrave house, we behave like Christians.
Therefore, we will love you as one of our own.

MORSE: Why?

*(DARCY takes the girl's other hand and the three of them
stand together. BUNCE stands alone.)*

DARCY: Because you're one of us.

(End Scene Two)

Scene Three

*(BUNCE sitting alone in the bare room. A key turns in a lock,
and an apple rolls across the stage towards him. He picks it
up, smells it with ecstasy. SNELGRAVE enters.)*

BUNCE: I haven't seen one of these in weeks.

SNELGRAVE: Something special I have Kabe bring in
now and then.

BUNCE: The three of you in the kitchen?

SNELGRAVE: For the time being.

(BUNCE holds up the apple, admires it, then begins to eat.)

SNELGRAVE: I'm not a cruel man, Bunce. But even under these conditions I can't just let you walk about. This is my home. Under my protection. The problem is you have the only suitable room in the house because it has a door that I can lock and now we must sleep on the kitchen floor. *(Beat)* And you smell awfully.

BUNCE: It's the tar, sir.

SNELGRAVE: Ah ha! A sailor. I knew it! It keeps the water out, the tar. And your buttons, of cheese or bone?

BUNCE: Wood, sir.

SNELGRAVE: That's unusual. I know a bit about the waters myself. I work for the Navy Board, just down the lane, on Seething. My friend Samuel and I, we control the largest commercial venture in the country, hmm. The Royal Dockyards.

BUNCE: They're as good as closed, sir.

SNELGRAVE: That's the curse of this plague. It's stopped all trade. There's not a merchant ship that's left the main port in months. Rats eating at the silks, damp at the pepper. You fellows out of work, selling spice and nutmeg on the streets. And starving. The lot of you.

(BUNCE *eats the apple core as well.*)

BUNCE: I sailed three cats and a hag before we unloaded at the main port. Half of the crew got sick and died. A crowd set fire to three flys unloading beside our rig. They said the ships were carrying the plague. The crew had to swim to shore. Those that weren't burned.

SNELGRAVE: What were your routes? Did you ship to Calcutta? Bombay?

BUNCE: Green waters of the Caribbean and back, mostly. Green water, green islands, green air, and all the colors of Port Royal.

SNELGRAVE: Port Royal. They say the women there are masculine and obscene.

BUNCE: Salt Beef Peg.

SNELGRAVE: Your wife, certainly?

BUNCE: Not married.

SNELGRAVE: *(Enjoying this)* Shameful.

BUNCE: She had nothing on Buttock-de-Clink Jenny.

SNELGRAVE: Not in this house.

BUNCE: Old Cunning-finger Nan. As sweet and sour as...ah well. Sorry, sir. There's not a lot of good memories a sailor has, and them he has he carries tucked deep in.

SNELGRAVE: I've heard the stories at the coffeehouse. You know, I often dream of the sea but if I step my foot in a boat, the world goes black before my eyes. My body can't abide it, but my heart. Well. *(Beat)* I'm a rich man, Bunce, and you a common sailor yet—look at the two of us—we have the sea between us. The struggle, the daring, the wrath. Cathay's lake of rubies. The North-West passage. Ice monsters fouling the sea— that angry bitch that'll tear you limb from limb. Man against the elements.

BUNCE: Mostly for us sailors it was man against the Captain.

SNELGRAVE: *(Begins to rock back and forth, eyes closed, living in the moment of a sea story)* And the winds, how they blow like a madness and the sea leaps up like a continuous flame. The hideous, howling wilderness that stabs at the hull, that would rend flesh from bone. Sea spouts the size of cities. The cargo shifting and tumbling below deck and water casks rolling from side to side. One terrible cry after another pierces the air as the crew is swept overboard.

(Motions for BUNCE to stand beside him and rock back and forth with him. After some initial hesitation, BUNCE does so)

SNELGRAVE: To lessen the resistance to the fiendish wind and keep her from capsizing, three of our best

crawl on deck with axes and climb aloft to cut away the
fore top mast and the bowsprit ropes.

BUNCE: And as they hack at the mast, a monstrous
wave, three times the size of the rig, whacks the
starboard and snaps the foremast like a stick, and
carries it with one of the sailors into the sea. The second
is crushed

SNELGRAVE: (*Continues for* BUNCE*)* between the mast
and the side of the ship.

BUNCE: The third is hung by his boot in the ratline.

SNELGRAVE: The sea has no mercy and smashes all who
try to rule her beneath her foul and lecherous waves.

BUNCE: Smashing, smashing.

SNELGRAVE: (*Continues*) Smashing the small vessel like
egg shells against a stone. Oh death, death, death.

(SNELGRAVE *whacks his stick on the floor furiously a few
times.*)

SNELGRAVE: And scurvy. Did you get the scurvy?

BUNCE: Many a time.

SNELGRAVE: Knots. You can do knots? (*Takes out a piece
of rope. Knots it.*) What's that?

BUNCE: That's a bowline. But your tail's too short.

SNELGRAVE: Is it?

(BUNCE *takes the rope and reties the knot.*)

SNELGRAVE: Hmmm. Show me another.

(BUNCE *does a series of knots, one after the other as they
speak.*)

BUNCE: Butterfly knot.

SNELGRAVE: (*Indicating a scar on* BUNCE's *neck*)
How'd you get that scar? Spanish Main pirates?!

BUNCE: (*Another knot*) Lighterman's hitch. (*Meaning his
neck*) Sail hook.

SNELGRAVE: In a drunken brawl?

BUNCE: We were a short ways outside Gravesend.
Our fly was carrying sugar and rum. The press gangs
were looking for fresh recruits and boarded us just
as we came into port. *(Another knot)* Half hitch with
seizing. *(Beat)* To keep from the press, sometimes we'd
cut ourselves a wound and then burn it with vitriol.
Make it look like scurvy. They wanted whole men,
so I stuck myself in the neck with a sail hook. They
passed me over when they saw the blood.

(SNELGRAVE *hands* BUNCE *some more nuts.* BUNCE *eats.*
SNELGRAVE *watches him eat.)*

(End Scene Three)

Scene Four

(MORSE, BUNCE, DARCY, *and* SNELGRAVE *in their room.*
DARCY *reads but more often just stares.* SNELGRAVE *sits*
with an unopened book. MORSE *sits and stares.* BUNCE *sits*
in the corner on a dirty mat, making himself small. A sense
of boredom, tedium inside a house where no one can leave.)

SNELGRAVE: Did you vinegar the corner, under your
mat, as well, Bunce?

BUNCE: Yes I did, sir.

SNELGRAVE: Right.

(Long silence)

SNELGRAVE: The chairs as well?

BUNCE: Yes, sir.

SNELGRAVE: Right.

MORSE: *(Sings)* Over and across the tall, tall grass
They lay my love in the dirt
He was just a kid and myself a lass
If it'd bring him back, I'd reconvert.

(SNELGRAVE *whacks his cane.)*

SNELGRAVE: Not in this house.

DARCY: Oh, let her sing.

MORSE: *(Continues)*
O fire of the devil, fire of love
The truth is a lie and the pig's a dove

SNELGRAVE: She doesn't sing like a Christian child.

MORSE: *(Continues)*
The desert is cold and Hell is hot
The mouth that kisses is sweet with rot.

DARCY: I don't think I've heard song in this house since—

MORSE: Can't you sing?

DARCY: I don't like to. But I like to hear it. Sometimes.

MORSE: Are you not hot in all that dress?

DARCY: No, child. I never wear anything but this sort of dress.

MORSE: Can I see your neck?

DARCY: What? Why, child?

MORSE: Because I think you must have a beautiful neck and it's the time of the plague and there's not much of beauty left in this city but you.

DARCY: Who taught you to lie so kindly?

MORSE: Learned it myself. Can I see?

DARCY: I will get you a looking glass and you can look at your own neck, which is lovely. Mine is not. I am old.

MORSE: Please.

SNELGRAVE: Leave my wife in peace.

MORSE: Let me see.

SNELGRAVE: Sit back down.

MORSE: I think you have the scar of the hangman about your neck.

SNELGRAVE: I said leave her be.

DARCY: She means no harm.

MORSE: Or perhaps the finger marks of someone who hates you.

DARCY: *(Laughing)* Perhaps the hole of a sword that went in here and came out there!

SNELGRAVE: Must you encourage such putrid imaginings? Enough. My head hurts from it.

(SNELGRAVE *exits.)*

DARCY: Stand here, child.

(MORSE *nears her.)*

DARCY: Closer. Let me feel your breath on my cheek.

(MORSE *moves closer.)*

DARCY: The breath of a child has passed through the lungs of an angel. That's what they say.

MORSE: My mother said to me that once a tiny piece of star broke off and fell from the sky while she slept in a field of wheat and it pierced her, here,

(Motions to DARCY's *heart but doesn't touch her)*

MORSE: and from that piece of star I was born.

DARCY: And your father. What did he say? That he molded you from a sliver of moon?

MORSE: My father is dead.

DARCY: I know. But what did he say about his little girl?

MORSE: My father was born dead. He stayed that way most of his life.

DARCY: I met your father, at the Opera, once. He seemed a decent man.

MORSE: My father hit the maids. I saw him do it. Sometimes twice a day.

DARCY: Well, then, he kept order. A household must have order.

MORSE: He used a piece of leg from a chair. He kept it in the drawer of his writing desk.

DARCY: Sometimes servants misbehave. That's not your father's fault.

MORSE: Do you hit your servants?

DARCY: My servants are dead.

MORSE: Did you hit them?

DARCY: No, I didn't. But when they did not listen, I told my husband and he dealt with them as was necessary.

MORSE: Can I see your neck now?

DARCY: No, you cannot.

MORSE: Can I see your hands?

DARCY: My hands are private.

MORSE: I'm not afraid to die.

DARCY: You don't have to be; you won't die.

MORSE: I already know what it's like. To be dead. It's nothing fancy.

(She moves away from DARCY. She takes the hem of her dress in her hands.)

MORSE: Just lots of nothing to see all around you and nothing to feel, only there's a sound that comes and goes. Comes and goes. Like this:

(She slowly tears a rip in her dress, up to her waist. We hear the sound of ripping cloth.)

MORSE: Have you heard that sound before, Mrs Snelgrave?

(DARCY does not answer. MORSE speaks now to BUNCE.)

MORSE: And you, sitting there on your lily pad like a frog? Have you heard it?

BUNCE: In Northumberland. Yeah. A coal miner I was, when I was a kid. We heard all sorts of things down in the earth. And when our lanterns went out, our minds went to hell.

MORSE: Did lots of you die down there?

DARCY: Morse.

BUNCE: Lost my baby brother in the mines. Well, he
wasn't a baby, but he always was to us. Just thirteen, he
was. We went deep for the coal. They kept pushing us.
Pushing us deeper. The ceilings were half down most of
the time. One fell in on top of us, six of us it were.

MORSE: Your brother was crushed?

BUNCE: Yes, he was. And the Master, he kicked me
'cause I was cursing the mine. I jumped him and his
men pulled me off. He kicked me again and I bit his ear
in two. One of his guards popped a knife in my side.
Never healed up right.

MORSE: What did he look like crushed up? Your brother.

DARCY: Stop it, Morse.

BUNCE: He looked like. Well. His face was the only part
of him. Not crushed. His face looked. I don't know.
What? Disappointed. I think.

DARCY: That's enough.

MORSE: *(To* BUNCE*)* And his body?

BUNCE: His body. It was like. What? Like water.
What was left of him. I couldn't take him up in my
arms. He just. Spilled away.

(MORSE *nears* BUNCE, *kneels down and simply looks at him.
After some moments,* BUNCE *looks away from her and at*
DARCY.)

(End Scene Four)

Scene Five

(Outside of the SNELGRAVES' *house. Just below the window.*
KABE *is guarding the house.)*

KABE: *(Calls)* Bills. The Bills. Stepney Parish, seven
hundred and sixteen. White-Chapel, three hundred
forty six. The Bills. St Giles's Cripplegate, two hundred
seventy-seven. St Leonard Shoreditch—

MORSE: *(Pops her head out of the window above him)*
I got an uncle in St Sepulchers. How's it there?

KABE: Two hundred and fourteen dead this week.
How's the Snelgraves?

MORSE: We're all right.

KABE: You a relative?

MORSE: Mrs Snelgrave says you're a thief.

KABE: Does she now? And how old are you, sweetheart?

MORSE: Twelve. Mr Snelgrave says you're the worst
sort of rabble.

KABE: We're always rabble, we are, when we come
out from our alleys and lanes and rub shoulders with
Snelgrave's, hawk an innocent gob o' phlegm on their
doorstep. They're not much company, how 'bout you?

MORSE: Mr Snelgrave says you're not much above
vermin.

KABE: Does he now? And have you ever seen a little
mousie?

MORSE: I seen rats.

KABE: Ever had a sweetheart?

(MORSE shakes her head 'no'.)

KABE: Doctors say virgins ripe for marriage are ripe
for the infection, their blood being hot and their seed
pining for copulation.

MORSE: Mr Snelgrave says you want us to die.
Then you can come in and loot.

KABE: I could show you a jewel that'd change your life.

MORSE: Go ahead then.

KABE: Don't know if you're grown enough.

MORSE: I'm old on the inside. Show me.

KABE: Hold onto that window.

(KABE stands directly under her and opens his pants.
MORSE looks. And looks.)

KABE: Well!

MORSE: You're a man, then?

KABE: Of course I'm a man. A bull of a man.
A whale of a man.

MORSE: Sometimes people pretend.

KABE: *(Closing his pants)* What you just saw wasn't
pretending.

MORSE: Don't like all the strawy hairs on it.

KABE: Have you no manners, you prince's whore?
You should be beaten. Have you ever been beaten?

MORSE: *(Laughing at him)* Lots of times. Can you get me
a Certificate of Health from the Lord Mayor so I can
pass out of the city?

KABE: *(Shrieks with laughter)* You're a card, aren't you!

MORSE: I'm dead serious.

KABE: He's no longer in town.

MORSE: Yes he is. Lord Mayor of London. He's the only
one who stayed.

KABE: Not counting the poor, child. The poor's all
stayed. And what I hear tell, that's not the Mayor in the
Mayor's house but a mad man who broke in and jumps
naked through the garden, cawing like a crow at night.
The rest of the Court's gone too. All that's got wealth
has fled from the plague. And God's followed them.

MORSE: The Snelgraves haven't fled.

KABE: That's not for trying. They just got unlucky; their
servants died before they could leave 'em behind to
starve.

MORSE: Get me a Certificate so I can pass the blockades.

KABE: I got ahold of a few of those papers at the very
start, but now. Well. They're as rare as.... And what
would you give me in return?

MORSE: Don't have much.

KABE: Let me have a feel of your leg. Go on.

MORSE: Why?

KABE: I've got an idea. Or two.

MORSE: (*Hangs a leg out the window*) There's my leg.

KABE: (*Feeling her leg*) A bit bony. I can't get you a Certificate even if I wanted, but—

(MORSE *starts to pull her leg back in, but he hangs on.*)

KABE: Wait! I can get you some sugar knots. I know an old man who's got a bucketful.

MORSE: Got no money.

KABE: I'll make you a deal. You let me, ah, kiss your foot and for every kiss I'll get you a sugar knot.

MORSE: Deal.

(KABE *kisses her foot, twice. Then sucks on her big toe.* MORSE *kicks him.*)

MORSE: You said kiss, not suck.

KABE: What's the difference?

MORSE: An apple. A suck is worth an apple.

KABE: Thief.

(*He sucks on her toe. Then she pulls her leg up*)

KABE: That was a nibble, not a suck!

MORSE: Two sugar knots and an apple. And the worms in the apple better be alive!

KABE: You'll die by the plague, child. I feel it in me shins.

MORSE: Then I'll be good at being dead. My father and mother are already dead. Poor Daddy. Poor Mommy. Dead, dead, dead.

KABE: Stupid brat. What you lack is fear. This past week, I got the bodies piled so high in my cart I could hardly see over the tops of them. (*Beat*) Hey. I know an old woman who's got tangerines, still good, that she wears under her skirts. She says they stay fresh down there because she's hot as the tropics.

MORSE: Get me a tangerine too.

KABE: Bring me a jewel of Mrs Snelgrave's. Anything. Just make sure the gem's hard.

MORSE: I'm not a Braithwaite anymore, you know.

KABE: And I am not a guard at your door. But if you crawl out of that window, I will kill you and sleep well this night.

MORSE: Perhaps I'll kill you first.

KABE: (Calling) The ninety-seven parishes within the walls: one thousand four hundred and ninety-three. Parishes on the Southwark Side: one thousand six hundred and thirty-six. (Sings)

We'll all meet in the grave
Then we'll all be saved.
You with your coins
Me with me scabs.
You with clean loins
Me with me crabs
We'll all meet in the grave
Then we'll all get laid down
Oh, down, deep down

(End Scene Five)

Scene Six

(BUNCE washes the floor with vinegar. He uses a small rag and a bucket. SNELGRAVE watches him.)

SNELGRAVE: I heard the crier this morning. The Bills have almost doubled this week. Mostly the Out Parishes of the poor. But it's moving this way. A couple of persons I know personally have died. Decent people. Good Christians on the surface. But there's the key.

On the surface. When the poor die, the beggars, it's no
riddle. Look down at their faces and you'll see their
bitter hearts. When the rich die, it's harder to tell why
God took them; they're clean, attend the Masses, give
alms. But something rotten lurks. Mark my words,
Bunce. A fine set of clothes does not always attest to
a fine set of morals.

(BUNCE, *wiping the floors, nears* SNELGRAVE's *shoes.*)

SNELGRAVE: Are you afraid, Bunce?

BUNCE: Sir?

SNELGRAVE: Are you afraid of the plague?

BUNCE: Who isn't, sir?

SNELGRAVE: It is written in the Ninety-First Psalm of
the Book: "Thou shalt not be afraid for the pestilence
that walketh in darkness... A thousand shall fall at thy
side, and ten thousand at thy right hand: but it shall not
come nigh thee." That doesn't mean I don't ever doubt,
Bunce. I use vinegar.

BUNCE: Those are fine shoes, sir. The finest I ever saw
this close up.

SNELGRAVE: Cost me as much as a silk suit. A bit tight
on my corns, but real gentlemen's leather. I would
wager your life, Bunce, that you'll never wear such fine
shoes as these.

BUNCE: I'd wager two of my lives, if I had them.

SNELGRAVE: A little learning, Bunce: Patterns will have
it that you, a poor sailor, will never wear such shoes as
these. And yet, the movement of history, which is as
inflexible as stone, can suddenly change. With a flick
of a wrist. Or, I might say, an ankle. Watch while I
demonstrate. (*He slips out of his shoes.*) Put them on,
Bunce.

BUNCE: Sir?

SNELGRAVE: Put my shoes on your feet.

BUNCE: My feet are dirty, sir.

SNELGRAVE: Then have my socks on first.

(BUNCE *holds up the fine socks and examines them.*)

SNELGRAVE: Go on, then.

(BUNCE *carefully slips on the socks, then the shoes. The two men stand side by side looking back and forth at their own and each other's feet.* SNELGRAVE *wiggles his bare toes.*)

SNELGRAVE: Now, Bunce. What do you see?

BUNCE: I see the Master is without shoes. And his new servant. He is wearing very fine shoes.

SNELGRAVE: And history? What does history tell you now?

BUNCE: Not sure how that works, sir.

SNELGRAVE: Historically speaking, the poor do not take to fine shoes. They never have and they never will.

BUNCE: I'm wearing fine shoes now.

SNELGRAVE: Yes, but only because I allow it. I have given history a wee slap on the buttocks and for a moment something terribly strange has happened: you in my shoes. However, what we see here is not real. It's an illusion because I can't change the fact that you'll never wear fine shoes.

BUNCE: But I'm wearing them now, sir.

SNELGRAVE: Only because I gave them to you. In a moment I am going to take them back, and then history will be on course again. As a matter of fact, it never strayed from course, because what we're doing here is just a little game.

BUNCE: What if I kept the shoes?

SNELGRAVE: Kept them? You can't keep them. They're mine.

BUNCE: I know they're yours, sir. I'm just asking what if I kept them?

SNELGRAVE: That's not a historical question.

BUNCE: No. It's a game question. You said this was a game, sir.

SNELGRAVE: So I did. Well, if you kept them I would go and get another pair before my feet got cold.

BUNCE: Then we'd both have a pair.

SNELGRAVE: You're not attacking the problem correctly. If we both have a pair, how will people tell our feet apart? They'll look the same. That's not history, Bunce, that's obfuscatory.

BUNCE: May I have your cane?

SNELGRAVE: You most certainly may not.

BUNCE: I just want to hold it, sir. It's finely carved. I'll never hold a cane like that in my life.

SNELGRAVE: *(He reluctantly hands it to him.)* I'm not a cruel man.

(BUNCE takes the cane, tucks it awkwardly under his arm.)

SNELGRAVE: Not like that. It's not a piece of firewood you're lugging for the stove.

(SNELGRAVE snatches is back. Delicately tucks it under his arm and walks this way and that.)

BUNCE: It doesn't look right on you without the shoes, sir.

(BUNCE holds out his hand and after a moment's hesitation, SNELGRAVE hands the cane to him. BUNCE carries the cane almost properly this time.)

SNELGRAVE: That's it. Elbow a bit higher. I always think of it as walking across the hands of children. You must do it lightly and carefully or you'll break their bones.

BUNCE: Is this it, sir? History?

SNELGRAVE: Certainly not. This is just practice.

BUNCE: Practice for what?

SNELGRAVE: Brrrrr. My feet are cold. The shoes, please.

(BUNCE *walks once more to and fro, then stops face to face with* SNELGRAVE, *close. Silence for some moments. He hands* SNELGRAVE *the cane and removes the shoes, slowly, then the socks. He sets the shoes carefully and neatly between them, laying out the socks one by one. The two men look at the shoes between them. They watch each other some moments, then* BUNCE *returns to his bucket and rag. He cleans.* SNELGRAVE *picks up his shoes and socks*).

SNELGRAVE: The Bills are up. Way up this week. We'll need to vinegar this room twice a day from now on. Starting tomorrow. One can't be too cautious. I'll send my wife in with some bread for you when you're done.

BUNCE: Yes, sir.

(SNELGRAVE *begins to exit.*)

BUNCE: Sir?

(SNELGRAVE *turns to hear him.*)

BUNCE: I'm not a cruel man, either, sir.

SNELGRAVE: I know that, Bunce. I wouldn't have taken you on as my servant if I had thought otherwise.

(SNELGRAVE *exits. We hear the lock turn.*)

(*End Scene Six*)

Scene Seven

(BUNCE *adjusting his wrappings under his shirt.* DARCY *enters, watches him some moments. He's unaware and curses the wrappings that are beginning to fall to pieces in his hands. We hear* KABE *singing offstage.*)

KABE: (*Sings*)
Calico, silk, porcelain, tea
It's all the same to the poor man and me

BUNCE: Ah, fuck the Lord.

KABE: (Sings, offstage)
Steal it in the Indies, haul it cross the sea
And now it's nothing between the plague, you and me.

BUNCE: Ow! Fuck his Angels too.

DARCY: I brought you some clean linen.

BUNCE: (Backing into his corner) Beg your pardon, Mrs.
I thought you three were asleep.

DARCY: They are. Does it hurt all the time?

BUNCE: Only when I sit a lot. On the sea I'm standing
most of the time and I feel best.

DARCY: Here's a clean shirt. It belonged to our servant
boy. I've soaked it in vinegar and cloves. It's safe.

BUNCE: (He takes the shirt.) Thank you, Mrs.

DARCY: I brought some clean strips too. So you can
rebind it.

BUNCE: (He takes them.) You're kind.

DARCY: I don't want blood on my floors.

(They each wait for something from the other.)

BUNCE: Perhaps you should go back to the kitchen, Mrs.

DARCY: I will stay.

BUNCE: It's not pretty.

(DARCY doesn't leave so BUNCE shrugs and painfully takes
off his old shirt. His old bandage is still in place. He begins to
wrap the new one over it.)

DARCY: Take the old one off or it will do no good to put
a clean one on.

BUNCE: It does no good anyhow but make it look better.

DARCY: I will do it.

BUNCE: No.

DARCY: (Taking the new bandage from him) Yes, I will.

BUNCE: (Angry, holding the old bandage in place) I said no,
Mrs.

DARCY: All right then. Do it yourself.

(She tosses the bandage at his feet so he must stoop to pick it up. He does so.)

BUNCE: *(Wanting her to turn away)* Please.

(She does so, annoyed. Turning his side with the wound away from her, he rebinds it. We do not see the wound, as he keeps it hidden.)

DARCY: So you're a sailor. Merchant or Navy?

BUNCE: Merchant by choice. Navy by force.

DARCY: Then it's the sailor's life for you: Drinking, thieving, whoring, killing, backbiting. And swearing.

BUNCE: *(Playing into the cliche)* Yeah. Swearing. And once or twice we took hold of our own fucked ship from some goddamned captain. We let our men vote if the bloody prick lived or died. Mostly our men voted he died so first we whipped and pickled him, then threw the fat gutted chucklehead overboard. And because we couldn't piss on his grave we pissed on the bastard's back as he sank to the sharks below.

DARCY: A tongue that swears does not easily pray.

BUNCE: The times I was asked by my Captain or his mate to beat a fellow tar? I can't count them. The times I refused? Maybe less than one.

(Some moments of silence)

DARCY: I've never sailed on a ship. I married when I was fifteen. *(Beat)* Why did you come to our house?

BUNCE: The ships aren't sailing but the Navy's. I didn't want to get picked up again.

DARCY: Some would consider it an honor to serve the Navy.

BUNCE: Ay. Some would. Though I never met them.

DARCY: Do you have a wife?

BUNCE: I did for a little while, but I lost her. Was coming into port at Liverpool, merchant ship. Making short trips. Got picked up for the second time to serve his Majesty's ships. Didn't get back to port for eight months, and then my wife was gone. If she still lives, I don't know. The neighbors said she raved for months and went mad. Tick fever. But I don't believe it. She was a smart one. I think she just got tired of waiting and moved on.

DARCY: Did your wife have soft. Skin?

BUNCE: Soft skin? Well, no. It wasn't what you'd call soft. Her father was a ribband weaver and she worked by his side. Her hands were harder than mine.

DARCY: I'm sorry.

BUNCE: She used them well.

DARCY: Have you never touched a woman's skin that was soft?

BUNCE: Not a woman's, no. But I met a lad in the port of Bristol once, and he had skin so fine it was like running your fingers through water.

DARCY: You speak against God.

BUNCE: I'm speaking of God's pleasure.

DARCY: (*Picking up the scraps of bandage he's discarded*) And his. Breast. Was it smooth as well?

BUNCE: His breast. It was. Darker. Like the skin of an apple it smelled, and as smooth.

DARCY: Did you love him?

BUNCE: For those few months I loved him better than I could love another in years. His name was Killigrew. We got picked up off the streets and pressed onto the same ship. Warred against the Hollanders. He died.

DARCY: I'm sorry.

BUNCE: The bastard. Always had the luck.

DARCY: *(Taking off her earrings)* When this is over and we're allowed to leave here, you'll have these. You'll be able to eat awhile and pay for shelter. They're real stones.

BUNCE: *(Accepting the earrings. Examining them.)* Why am I to be paid like this?

DARCY: It's not payment. It's charity.

BUNCE: I'm poor, Mrs, but not stupid. If your husband catches me with these I might as well jump into the pits.

DARCY: He won't find them if you keep them well hid.

BUNCE: Hid where? You keep 'em. When we're all out and by our own legs, if you still feel moved to charity, you can give them to me once more.

(He hands them back. She puts them on again.)

DARCY: And this man you loved. Killigrew. Were his.

BUNCE: What.

DARCY: *(She touches her own thighs. Not in a seductive manner, but as though she can't bring herself to say the word out loud.)* Here. Was he smooth here?

BUNCE: What do you want, Mrs?

DARCY: For you to answer me.

BUNCE: And if I don't?

DARCY: We no longer lock you up. We trust you now.

BUNCE: All right. *(He nears her, close.)* Close your eyes. I'll do you no harm.

(DARCY closes her eyes. BUNCE softly blows air across her face. When he stops, she does not open her eyes.)

BUNCE: That's how it felt to touch him there.

(Some moments of silence)

DARCY: I don't intend to die of the plague, Bunce. My husband has agreed to help me end my life if the tokens appear.

BUNCE: Not all that gets the plague dies.

DARCY: First the marks appear around the neck or groin. There's fever. Violent vomiting. The patient cannot control the body. The body fouls itself.

BUNCE: But if the swelling can be brought to break and run, sometimes a person can live. I saved a friend that way once. Cut the marks with a knife and bled them. He never could speak again, but he lived.

DARCY: No, no. The stench of the sores is unbearable. The body rots. And then the mind. Lunacy and madness is the end. I saw two of our servants die that way. Their screams are locked inside my head forever.

BUNCE: Would you like to know of any other parts of my lad Killigrew, Mrs?

DARCY: No. Thank you. I've heard enough. Just bless the Lord He's brought you into this house. Against our will, certainly, but I assume not against His. *(Beat)* I could have you hanged for speaking of such matters to a married woman of my position.

BUNCE: *(Sings)* Lust in his limbs and rust in his skin A bear without, and a worse beast within.

DARCY: I'm just an old woman. That's what you think. Well. Smile as you like. I once had a lover, and his arms were so strong that my skull was crushed in his grip. With his bare hands he plunged between my ribs and took hold of my heart. A wafer between his fingers, it dissolved. Sometimes I wake up in the dark and stand in the hall and I can feel the cold draft pass freely through my chest as though there were nothing there.

BUNCE: I'll have those earrings after all.

(DARCY is motionless, as though not hearing him. He gently slips the earrings from her ears.)

BUNCE: I'll find a place. I'm a pirate.

(End Scene Seven)

Scene Eight

(DARCY, MORSE, *and* SNELGRAVE *in the room.* MORSE's *wrists are bound with rope.*)

SNELGRAVE: The child's a thief, I tell you. What did I find in her pockets one morning last week? A set of my Spanish gold coins. "Just playing jacks with them" she says. She's got the manners of a servant and the tongue of a who—

DARCY: Don't you dare.

SNELGRAVE: That brooch belonged to my mother. Not you. The child will confess when I give her some of this.

(SNELGRAVE *brandishes his cane.*)

DARCY: I'll find the brooch. It's bound to have fallen when I was turning things out.

SNELGRAVE: The child will wear those ropes until we find it.

MORSE: I didn't steal your brooch.

SNELGRAVE: Hold your tongue.

MORSE: You belong in a cold, cold grave.

(SNELGRAVE *raises his cane to hit* MORSE. *She runs to hide behind* DARCY.)

MORSE: Help me, Mrs Snelgrave.

DARCY: You did steal his coins.

(SNELGRAVE *whacks and misses.*)

MORSE: Yes, I did. But you gave Bunce some of his gin.

SNELGRAVE: She did what?

MORSE: I saw it with my own eyes, sir. Mrs Snelgrave thought I was asleep. You were, but I wasn't and she poured some of your gin into a bowl and she took it to him. She watched him drink it.

SNELGRAVE: Is this true?

MORSE: *(Makes the sound)* Slurp, slurp.

DARCY: He asked me the other day if we might spare some spirits. I said no. Later, I changed my mind.

SNELGRAVE: In the middle of the night?

DARCY: I didn't want to wake you.

SNELGRAVE: *(To* MORSE*)* And what else did you see, Morse Braithwaite?

*(*MORSE *raises her roped hands to him. After a moment he understands the deal and takes off the ropes.)*

MORSE: She asked him if the new bandage fit right. He said it felt a bit tight. He asked her to feel it.

SNELGRAVE: He asked her to feel what?

DARCY: This is ridiculous.

SNELGRAVE: You. Felt his bandage?

DARCY: I merely checked his bandage to make sure it wasn't pressing the wound.

SNELGRAVE: You did this. How?

MORSE: I can show you.

SNELGRAVE: *(To* DARCY*)* How did you check his bandage?

*(*DARCY *doesn't answer, just shakes her head.* SNELGRAVE *calls* BUNCE.*)*

SNELGRAVE: Bunce. Bunce!

*(*BUNCE *enters with the rag and pail.)*

BUNCE: I haven't finished the kitchen walls yet, sir.

SNELGRAVE: Put down the vinegar. I want you to stand there. Right here. Yes. Nothing else. Just stand.

*(*BUNCE *stands with his back to the public.)*

SNELGRAVE: Now, Mrs Snelgrave. As my wife. As a Christian woman, show me how you checked that his bandage wasn't too tight. So that it wouldn't press the wound. *(Beat)* Do it, woman, or so help me what I do to him will not be worse than what I do to you.

(DARCY slowly nears BUNCE.)

SNELGRAVE: Just a minute, my dear. Surely, in the dark, his belly full of my gin, it would be difficult to feel the tension of his. Bandage. With your glove on. You must have taken off one of your gloves, didn't you? *(Whispers, with menace)* Didn't you?

MORSE: Yes, she did. Because her glove dropped on the floor as he was slurping the gin. Slurp, slu—

SNELGRAVE: *(To MORSE)* You shut your mouth. *(To DARCY)* Take off your glove. Let our good servant Bunce see what's touched him in the dark.

DARCY: William.

SNELGRAVE: Darcy?

(DARCY stands before BUNCE and removes her glove. We cannot see her bare hand as BUNCE is blocking our view.)

SNELGRAVE: Have a look, Bunce.

(BUNCE does not look down at her hand but looks at SNELGRAVE.)

BUNCE: If Mrs Snelgrave wishes to keep her hands private, sir, it's—

SNELGRAVE: *(To DARCY)* Tell him you want him to look. Because you do, don't you? That's the nature of secrets. They yearn to be exposed.

DARCY: You may. Look.

BUNCE: If it pleases you, Mrs.

DARCY: It does.

(BUNCE looks down at her hand. He does not react. Then he looks at SNELGRAVE, who deflates. MORSE slowly comes around BUNCE to have a look. She's amazed rather than disgusted. She backs away and turns to SNELGRAVE.)

MORSE: You did this to her!

SNELGRAVE: It was an accident.

MORSE: You did this.

(DARCY *puts her glove back on.)*

SNELGRAVE: *(Calm now)* No, child. It was the fire did
it to her. When she was seventeen. Just two years after
we married. We lived outside the city then. There was
a fire in the stables. She insisted on saving her horse.
It was a wedding gift.

MORSE: *(To* DARCY*)* Did you save the horse?

DARCY: No.

SNELGRAVE: She burned. My beautiful wife, who only
the night before I'd held in my arms. Naked, she was—

DARCY: Quiet, William.

SNELGRAVE: I used to kneel at your feet, by the bedside
at night.

(BUNCE *steps back and stands beside* MORSE. *They watch
the* SNELGRAVES.)

SNELGRAVE: And you'd let your robe fall open.
Your skin was like. Like. There wasn't a name for
it on this earth.

(DARCY *puts her gloved hand on his head, she comforts him
almost automatically. He closes his eyes.)*

SNELGRAVE: For hours on end in the night. My God,
how I loved you.

DARCY: *(She moves away from* SNELGRAVE.) Some of the
animals freed themselves. The dappled mare my father
gave me broke out of her stall. Her mane was on fire.
She kept leaping and rearing to shake it off but she
couldn't shake it off. The mare ran in circles around the
garden. Faster and faster she ran, the fire eating its way
to her coat. Her coat was wet, running with sweat, but
that didn't stop the fire from spreading out across her
flanks. A horse on fire. In full gallop. It was almost.
Beautiful. It would have been. Beautiful. But for the

smell. I can still smell them. After thirty-six years.
The horses. Burning.

(MORSE *puts her hand in* BUNCE's *hand, and the two of
them stand watching the* SNELGRAVES. *This action should
be a subtle, almost unconscious gesture, on both their parts.*)

(*End Scene Eight*)

Scene Nine

(KABE *outside on the street below the* SNELGRAVES' *window.
He is half-naked and wears a pan of burning charcoal on his
head. He is preaching.*)

KABE: A monster, last week, was born at Oxford in the
house of an Earl. His name on fear of death I do
withhold. One eye in its forehead, no nose, and its two
ears in the nape of its neck. And outside in the garden
of that very same house, a thorn which bore five
different fruits. And, good people of this city, if we
must read these phenomena as signs—

SNELGRAVE: (*At the window*) Kabe.

KABE: And we must. Listen not to the liars and
hypocrites—

SNELGRAVE: Did you get the quicksilver?

KABE: —for they will tell you that it is the wrath of God
against an entire people, corrupt in both spirit and in
heart.

(KABE *stops preaching, steps back, and speaks to*
SNELGRAVE.)

Got it. Babel, Babylon, Sodom and Gomorrah, cow shit I
tell you.

SNELGRAVE: And the walnut shell?

KABE: Had a little trouble with the walnut shell.
Hazelnut is all I could come by.

SNELGRAVE: A hazelnut shell? Have you gone mad?
Dr Brooks's pamphlet specifically states that the
quicksilver must be hung about the neck in a walnut
shell.

KABE: With the hazelnut, only five shillings.

SNELGRAVE: You said four yesterday.

KABE: That was before the Bills went up again. *(Turns
back to preach)* And I say to you if it is God's wrath, then
why has He chosen Oxford for the birth of this monster?

SNELGRAVE: What about the oil and frankincense?

KABE: Because Oxford is where the Court has retired,
the King and all his fancy, fawning courtiers. Because
the plague— *(To* SNELGRAVE*)* Couldn't get any—
(Preaching) is a Royalist phenomenon. Who dies? One
simple question. *(To* SNELGRAVE*)* But I do have a toad.
(Preaching) Who dies? *(To* SNELGRAVE*)* Not dead two
hours. *(Preaching)* Is this not a poor man's plague?
(To SNELGRAVE*)* Bore a hole through its head and
hang it about your neck.

SNELGRAVE: What if my wife spies it?

KABE: Keep it under your shirts. Should dry out in a
day or two.

SNELGRAVE: Two shillings.

KABE: Right. *(Preaching)* Go to the deepest pit near
Three Nuns' Inn, if you dare, and you will see who
it is that dies, their mouths open in want, the maggots
moving inside their tongues, making their tongues wag
as though they were about to speak. But they will never
speak again in this world. The hungry. The dirty. The
abandoned. That's who dies. Not the fancy and the
wealthy, there's hardly a one, for they have fled,
turned their back on the city. Clergymen, physicians
and surgeons, all fled.

SNELGRAVE: Have you thought again about my little
offer?

KABE: *(To* SNELGRAVE*)* Sorry.

SNELGRAVE: I could make you rich.

KABE: As well as dead if I let you escape. *(Preaching)*
And here we perish on the streets in such vast number
as much from lack of bread and wages as from the
plague—

SNELGRAVE: Where are your clothes? And what's that
you got on your head?

KABE: Pan of charcoal. Keeps the bad air from my head
when I unplug my finger from God's arsehole.

SNELGRAVE: Blasphemer! Put on your clothes. You're a
Snelgrave Guard.

KABE: Not on Tuesdays I'm not. *(Nods to offstage)* On
Tuesdays old Stewart fills in for me.

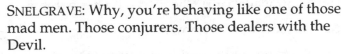

SNELGRAVE: Why, you're behaving like one of those
mad men. Those conjurers. Those dealers with the
Devil.

KABE: Solomon Eagle, at your service.

SNELGRAVE: This is outrageous. I won't have a conjurer
guarding our door! It's bad enough that I'm kept
captive by you, Kabe, but that you summon more
scum from their hellholes to stand below my windows.
My house. My street. My city!

KABE: *(Preaches again)* —is on the verge of the eternal
storm of chaos. Orphan's money is on loan by the Lord
Mayor to the King, and Parliament takes no action.
They stir their soup with our bones. The grass grows up
and down White Hall court and no boats move on the
river but to war. Dead as dung upon the face of the
earth we all shall be if we do not resist. I say to you:
Get off your knees. Rise up! Rise up! *(Beat)* But how
do we begin? With this. With this, my friends. *(He takes
out a small vial of liquid.)* The road to the Poor Man's
Heaven: only six shillings! Solomon Eagle's
plague-water.

SNELGRAVE: Six shillings! That's robbery.

KABE: *(Preaching still)* Is your dignity not worth six
shillings? It's your duty to keep your body strong for
this long and bloody struggle! Do not let the Monsters
of Oxford beat you down. Arise, arise into all your
glory! You, the mob! The dissolute rabble! Six shillings!
Six shillings, and the world is yours!

SNELGRAVE: I'll give you five.

(Drops the coins to KABE, *who catches them in a small jar of
vinegar)*

SNELGRAVE: Do I drink it?

KABE: One thimbleful each night before retiring. Also
anoint the nostrils, ear holes and anus twice a day.
(Beat) Sir Braithwaite's girl. She died with her parents.

SNELGRAVE: How do you know?

KABE: Spoke to one of the maids that used to work
there. Her husband did their garden. He found the
family dead. They say there was something stuffed
in the dead child's mouth. Some kind of animal.

SNELGRAVE: She can't be dead! She's alive and well and
a pest in my house.

KABE: The maid used to bathe the Braithwaite girl.
Maid said the girl had a scar the shape of a key 'cross
her belly. Happened when she was a baby. Some kind
of accident. *(Beat)* I've been thinking, sir. If one of you
dies in there, can we pull the body out the window?
We doubled up the boards on your door and it will be
a hell of a work to open it up again.

SNELGRAVE: The dying is done in this house, I thank the
Lord. And when the dying is done in this city, Kabe,
you better run, because I smell a Leveller's blood in
you, ringing loud and clear. I thought we buried the
lot of you.

KABE: My father was a Leveller, sir. His son's just a poor man with a pan of charcoal on his head. And now the old man's dead.

SNELGRAVE: Plague?

KABE: One of my toads, sir. Had a dozen of them in a bucket at the bedside. One of them got out and, well, my father, he snored and down one went and got stuck and the old man choked to death.

SNELGRAVE: A proper death for a man of his station. Levellers. Diggers. I say cut them to pieces or they will cut us to pieces.

KABE: Do you want the toad as it is, or do you want me to bore the hole?

SNELGRAVE: You do it. And get me a piece of string to hang it on as well.

KABE: Wife's piss also works wonders.

SNELGRAVE: *(Realizing he's being taken in)* Vermin.

KABE: Use your wife's urine to purify, before that sailor does.

SNELGRAVE: You'll be dead soon...

KABE: But will she let you have it?

SNELGRAVE: And I'll find you in your lime pit and piss in your mouth.

(End Scene Nine)

Scene Ten

(SNELGRAVE, DARCY, MORSE, and BUNCE in the room. Boredom. MORSE sits and ties figures out of cloth and sticks. Then she glances about the room. Her eyes rest on DARCY. She stands and goes to her.)

MORSE: I can smell your heart.

DARCY: Can you?

MORSE: It's sweet. It's rotting in your chest.

(SNELGRAVE *snorts.*)

MORSE: My mother didn't smell like you. She smelled like lemons.

DARCY: That's lovely.

MORSE: Because she was always afraid.

(SNELGRAVE *snorts again.*)

MORSE: Last night I dreamed that an angel tried to land on our roof. But he had no feet so he couldn't stand. He crawled in through the window, to touch our faces, but he had no hands. He said to me 'Come to my arms.' But he had none. This morning I woke up and there was a feather in my mouth. Look.

(*She shows* DARCY *a small, white feather. She runs the feather gently over* DARCY's *face.*)

SNELGRAVE: Must we listen to this senseless babble day in and day out. I'm sick of it. Bloody sick of it.

DARCY: Then pass your time in the kitchen.

SNELGRAVE: Kabe says Sir Braithwaite's daughter died in her own house. Says they found her naked. Naked and dead. Stripped.

DARCY: Kabe is a liar.

MORSE: He showed me his mouse.

SNELGRAVE: He says the daughter had a scar. Under her skirts.

DARCY: A scar?

SNELGRAVE: On her stomach.

MORSE: (*To* DARCY) Is the rest of your body burned?

DARCY: Yes.

MORSE: What does it feel like?

SNELGRAVE: I think we should have a look.

DARCY: Feel like? Most of the places on my skin I can't feel.

(MORSE *runs her hand lightly down* DARCY's *arm, slowly.*)

MORSE: Can you feel that?

DARCY: No. Yes. There. At the elbow.

(MORSE *caresses* DARCY's *neck through the cloth.*)

SNELGRAVE: She's strong, but Bunce could manage.

DARCY: Yes. There. *(Beat)* Not there. No. Maybe. No.

SNELGRAVE: Bunce could do it.

(MORSE *runs her hands slowly over* DARCY's *breasts.*
DARCY *does not stop her. This action is no different from
how* MORSE *touched* DARCY's *arms.* SNELGRAVE *stands
over them.*)

MORSE: Can you feel this?

SNELGRAVE: A scar the shape of a key.

DARCY: *(Sincerely trying to answer* MORSE's *questions)*
Not yet. Yes. There. Under your left hand. I can feel
something there.

MORSE: What do you feel?

SNELGRAVE: We could all be in danger.

DARCY: I feel...I don't know. No one has touched me
there. In years.

SNELGRAVE: *(Grabbing* MORSE's *arm)* It's about time we
found out just who you are, young lady. Bunce!

DARCY: Let go of her.

SNELGRAVE: *(Shoving the child into* BUNCE's *arms)*
You're the strongest, Bunce. Strip her.

BUNCE: I don't think I should be the one, sir.

SNELGRAVE: You do as I tell you.

BUNCE: Will you show him your belly, Morse?

(MORSE *shakes her head but does not physically resist.
She is calm.*)

BUNCE: I'm sorry, then.

(BUNCE *begins to unbutton* MORSE's *shirt buttons.*)

DARCY: Bunce. Don't you dare.

(BUNCE *looks from* SNELGRAVE *to* DARCY.)

SNELGRAVE: You cross me?

DARCY: I sponged the child. Twice. She has the scar.
But your idiot Kabe is mistaken. It's not a key. The scar
is like a spoon. *(To* SNELGRAVE*)* After the fire. Not once.
Not even to embrace me. I was. Even changed. I was
still—

SNELGRAVE: *(Interrupts)* How could I have loved you?
It was never about who you were but about what was
left of you.

(MORSE, *raising her skirts to reveal her stomach, which has
no scar.)*

MORSE: The angel took my scar.

(SNELGRAVE *glares at his wife.)*

MORSE: In exchange for the feather.

BUNCE: I think I'll vinegar the kitchen walls again, sir.

(SNELGRAVE *puts out his cane to stop* BUNCE.)

SNELGRAVE: Tell me something, Bunce. If you had a
wife and she lied to you. Lied to you, in front of
company. What would you do?

(BUNCE *is silent.)*

SNELGRAVE: You'll learn, Bunce.

(SNELGRAVE *shoves* BUNCE *towards* DARCY, *accidentally
touching* BUNCE's *wound.* BUNCE *winces.* SNELGRAVE
looks at his hand in disgust and then wipes it off.)*

SNELGRAVE: Get that thing to stop oozing! There she is.
The liar. And perhaps a whore. Though she'd have to
do all her whoring in the dark because. Well. As a
young woman she was rather large up top. How would
you sailors say it?

BUNCE: Well-rigged, sir.

SNELGRAVE: Yes. As a young woman she was
well-rigged. Let's just say that half her sails have been
burned away and leave it at that. *(Beat)* As you stand
there, Bunce, looking at your wife, you realize that she's
not only a liar but unsound under all that linen. *(Beat)*
Strike her. *(Beat)* I said strike her.

BUNCE: *(To DARCY, because he is going to hit her)* I'm
sorry, Mrs. *(He raises his arm to strike her.)*

MORSE: *(Sinking to her knees, quietly)* Mother? *(Beat)*
Hush, hush. Do not cry.

*(The others look at her. MORSE has wet herself. She is ill.
The piss slowly makes a line across the floor between them.)*

MORSE: I am filled. With angels.

(End Scene Ten)

Scene Eleven

*(MORSE still sitting on the floor, alone, in dim light. In the
cell or place of confinement, as in Scene One.)*

MORSE: *(Whispers)* I can't. I can't remember.

(Sound of a slap. This time MORSE flinches at the slaps.)

MORSE: She smelled. Of lemons.

(Another slap, harder)

MORSE: Maybe she was my age. No. She was. Lissa was.
A year younger. She had brown hair as long as a
horse's tail and like cakes her dresses were. Rimmed
with yellows and blues. Lissa had a fat stick that she
kept in her trunk of toys and she would sneak up
behind me as I swept the floors and hit me across the
back. When I cried, she'd let me hold the bird that her
grandfather brought home with him from India. It was
a green and black bird and it could sing a melody.
When I held it I could feel its tiny heart beating inside
its chest.

(DARCY *enters and stands in the shadows of the cell.*)

MORSE: Sometimes when Lissa's father scolded her she would come running to me and fling herself into my arms and weep. Her tears soaked my dirty frock. (*After some moments she gets to her feet and feels her dress is wet.*) Ugh. I've wet myself. (*She takes the dress off and casts it in the corner. She is wearing long underwear, perhaps a boy's, underneath.*) And then I got sick and Mr Snelgrave shouted "Plague! Plague!," but I had no tokens.

(DARCY *takes up the dress and holds it, then exits with the dress.*)

MORSE: My teeth swelled. I vomited. I had the spotted fever. For three days, Mrs Snelgrave held me in her arms. (*Beat*) That week Kabe said the pits were near overflowing. But Kabe said it wasn't only the dead that went to the pits. Some of the living went to the pits to die of grief. More than once, he said, when he tried to pull the grievers out of the pits he heard a sound like a stick snapping in their chests.

Lissa's father, Mr Braithwaite, died first. Then the mother. They died quickly. In each other's arms. From inside out they rotted. Lissa died more slowly. We were alone in the house. She said, "Hold me." Her body was covered in tokens. (*Beat*) But it wasn't Lissa's blood that was on my sleeve. (*Beat*) Who was alive and who was dead? In the pits their faces looked the same. Dried out by grief. And their hearts snapping in two inside their chests. Such a sound, Kabe said. Such a small, small sound, like this: (*Makes a small sound.*)

(*End Scene Eleven*)

END ACT ONE

ACT TWO

Scene One

(SNELGRAVE *and* BUNCE *in the room*)

SNELGRAVE: And what was the longest period you sailed without port?

BUNCE: Two years. Though we docked, we couldn't leave the ship, so afraid was our Captain that we'd not come back.

SNELGRAVE: You're still a young man.

BUNCE: I was never a young man, sir.

SNELGRAVE: Well, in the name of God, what did you do with your natural instincts while so long at sea?

BUNCE: Stayed alive. As best we could.

SNELGRAVE: I mean with your baser instincts. Those instincts against God.

BUNCE: Aboard the vessels I sailed, we never murdered our Captain. Though once we threw one overboard after he beat the cook with a pitch mop.

SNELGRAVE: Bunce. You are in my house. I come in contact with the Court and Parliament. I attend Cabinet meetings. At this very moment the Dutch are nuzzling at our shores.

(*Gives* BUNCE *an orange, which* BUNCE *takes but does not eat.* BUNCE *lets out a whistle as oranges are a delicacy even in good times.*)

SNELGRAVE: On these long voyages, without the comforts of a wife, what did you do to satisfy your unseemly satisfactions?

BUNCE: Between the Devil and the deep blue sea, there's little satisfaction, sir.

SNELGRAVE: *(Whacks his cane)* At night, Bunce. Packed in there man to man, godforsaken flesh to godforsaken flesh. You're halfway to Madras and it's sweltering hot and you wake with the hunger of a shark. But not for food. The Devil is foaming at your lips. What do you do, man? You're frothing with desire. What do you do?

BUNCE: I don't know as I ever frothed with desire, sir.

SNELGRAVE: The Lord, may He be forgiven, Bunce, gave you a foul and fleshful instrument that resides in your loins. And though you may attempt to ignore this instrument of debasement, in the darkness of a ship, among the sweat of rats and tired men, this instrument certainly led you—

BUNCE: *(Interrupts)* You mean my prick, sir?

SNELGRAVE: Not in this house.

BUNCE: It goes where I go, sir.

SNELGRAVE: Exactly. And where does it go when your body is snarling and gnashing and snapping like a wild dog and it must be satisfied or you'll die!?

(BUNCE is silent.)

SNELGRAVE: God curse you! Speak!

(BUNCE nears SNELGRAVE, close, too close. He takes SNELGRAVE's finger, examines it a moment, and then forces it through the rind of the orange. BUNCE turns the orange on SNELGRAVE's finger, slowly, sensually. Then he pulls the orange off of SNELGRAVE's finger. Involuntarily, SNELGRAVE looks at his wet finger. BUNCE raises the orange over his head, squeezes it and drinks from the hole in the rind.)

SNELGRAVE: I issue commissions to the Navy Board.
(Beat) I draft resolutions to send to the king.

(They look at each other.)

(End Scene One)

Scene Two

*(SNELGRAVE, DARCY, MORSE, and BUNCE in the room.
MORSE now sits on the mat in the corner with BUNCE.
MORSE is in long johns. DARCY coughs once, twice.)*

BUNCE: Can I get you some water?

DARCY: No, thank you, Bunce.

SNELGRAVE: *(Mocking)* Can I get you some water?
Can I get you some water? What's happened to your
manners? It's Mrs Snelgrave. Mrs Snelgrave. Can I get
you some water, Mrs Snelgrave. *(Beat)* Bunce.

BUNCE: Mrs Snelgrave.

SNELGRAVE: That's right. That's right.

DARCY: William.

SNELGRAVE: I'm an old man, Bunce. I sleep sound.
Do you sleep sound?

BUNCE: Usually, sir.

SNELGRAVE: They say a man who'd put to sea for
pleasure would go to hell for pastime. *(Beat)* What's
your pastime, Bunce? Heh?

*(He begins to poke at BUNCE with his stick. MORSE runs to
DARCY.)*

SNELGRAVE: We'll be out of here one day. Never see
each other's rotten faces again. But where will you go?
What will you do? I have work. I have friends. Do you
have work, Bunce? Do you have friends?

MORSE: I'm his friend.

SNELGRAVE: *(To* MORSE*)* Ha. You're just a flea. *(Beat)*
Tell us another story, Bunce. A real brute of a sea story.
We've got some time left. To kill. I'll give you two
shillings if it's good.

BUNCE: No, sir.

SNELGRAVE: No?

MORSE: He said no.

SNELGRAVE: What's the matter, Bunce? What's got
under your skin?

(Poking him again with his stick, harder)

SNELGRAVE: What's on your mind?

BUNCE: I got four things on my mind, sir.

SNELGRAVE: *(Still poking him)* Go on. I'm intrigued.
Four things.

BUNCE: First is that stick you keep poking me with.
Second is when I get out of here, I won't sail for the
Navy again. Ever. I'll kill somebody first, even if it's me.
Third is your wife, Darcy Snelgrave. And fourth is your
wife as well. I count her twice cause she's much on my
mind—

SNELGRAVE: You filthy— How dare you think of my
wife!

BUNCE: You don't, sir, so I thought I might.

SNELGRAVE: What? What? What do you think of my
wife?

DARCY: Stop this, William.

SNELGRAVE: What do you think of my wife?

BUNCE: The way a tar thinks, sir, you don't want to
know.

SNELGRAVE: *(Still poking him)* No. I don't. You swine.
Eat your words. Eat them.

*(*SNELGRAVE *forces the stick in* BUNCE's *mouth.)*

SNELGRAVE: Eat them.

(BUNCE *firmly but calmly grabs the stick and walks*
SNELGRAVE *backwards until* SNELGRAVE *sits in his chair.)*

BUNCE: Move, sir, from this chair and I'll push this stick
through your heart.

SNELGRAVE: Darcy?

DARCY: *(Calmly)* Morse, bring me the rope.

SNELGRAVE: Darcy!

(MORSE *gets rope and they wrap it around* SNELGRAVE *and
tie him in the chair. Banging at the window.* BUNCE *pulls a
knife and warns* SNELGRAVE. KABE *pops his head in.)*

KABE: A morning to all, good neighbors. Mr Snelgrave,
Mrs Snelgrave. Rabble. Want the Bills this week? Not
leveling out. God save the King I say. The Devil won't
have him.

MORSE: We're playing: We're going to cook Mr
Snelgrave.

KABE: No harm done, heh? And here's something for
your game, Morse.

(He throws her an orange.)

KABE: Mrs Snelgrave? Need anything?

(There is no reply but an awkward silence.)

KABE: Well. I'm off, as the scab said. Working the pits.
Deaf Stewart'll take over for me tonight. Throw
something at him when you want his attention.

MORSE: Can you get me some good linen from the pits?
I want a new dress.

KABE: There's a king's ransom in them pits. And along
the roads. Bodies just asking you to strip 'em. If the
family ain't robbed them first. Probably before they
died...

DARCY: Morse! Kabe! Have you no sympathy...

KABE: They don't need it anymore, do they,
Mrs Snelgrave. Mr Snelgrave.

SNELGRAVE: Kabe...

KABE: *(Ignoring* SNELGRAVE's *plea)* What's terrible at the pits isn't the dead. What's terrible is that there are persons who aren't dead but are infected with the plague and they come freely to the pit, shouting, delirious with fever, half-naked, wrapped in blankets, and they throw themselves into the pits, on top of the dead, and expire there.

SNELGRAVE: Kabe!

KABE: Others are still dying. They leap about the pit, roaring, tearing the clothes from their bodies, taking up sticks and sharp stones and cutting open their sores to relieve the pain, some hacking away at their flesh until they fall down dead in their own blood. Ay, that's what's terrible. Not death, but life that has nothing left but still won't give itself up.

*(*KABE *waves and is gone.)*

SNELGRAVE: Let me go.

*(*BUNCE *begins removing* SNELGRAVE's *shoes.)*

SNELGRAVE: What in God's name are you doing?

*(*BUNCE *puts on the shoes.)*

BUNCE: I'm practicing.

*(*MORSE *puts the orange in* SNELGRAVE's *mouth.)*

(End Scene Two)

Scene Three

(Night. BUNCE *sits on his mat in the corner, watching over* SNELGRAVE, *who sleeps, still tied to his chair.* DARCY *enters. They watch each other silently in the dark.)*

DARCY: He sleeps.

BUNCE: Yes.

(After some moments)

BUNCE: What do you want, Mrs?

DARCY: I want. To see it.

BUNCE: Why?

DARCY: I think about it. All the time. What it must. Look like.

BUNCE: That's what you think about?

DARCY: Please. Lift your shirt.

BUNCE: You know what I think about, Mrs Snelgrave?

DARCY: Maybe it's a joke. A lie. And when you leave here you'll go out in the streets and pretend you're Christ, with a wound that doesn't heal, and they'll give you alms.

BUNCE: Excuse me, but it's none of your damn business.

(DARCY *turns to leave.*)

BUNCE: Darcy.

DARCY: You're not to call me that. Ever.

BUNCE: I don't want you to see it. *(Beat)* But you can touch it. If you must.

DARCY: Yes.

BUNCE: Give me your hand.

(She does so.)

BUNCE: Close your eyes, Mrs.

(DARCY *closes her eyes.*)

BUNCE: Keep them closed.

(She nods. He guides her hands under his shirt.)

BUNCE: Feel it?

DARCY: *(After some moments)* There.

BUNCE: Yeah.

DARCY: It's a small. Hole. Does it hurt?

BUNCE: I don't know. Some of the skin, it has feeling left. Go on. Some of it doesn't.

DARCY: There.

BUNCE: *(Winces, almost imperceptibly)* What?

DARCY: My finger. I've put my finger. Inside. It's warm. *(Beat)* It feels like I'm inside you.

BUNCE: You are.

(After some moments, DARCY takes her hand out from under his bandage. There is blood on her fingers. She looks at her hand as though it might be changed.)

DARCY: You should have died from a wound like that.

BUNCE: It was an accident.

DARCY: An accident?

BUNCE: That I lived.

DARCY: Do you know I've hardly given you a thought in these weeks, but every night I ravish you in my sleep. Why is that, Bunce? Can you tell me why that is?

BUNCE: It's nothing to worry over, Mrs Snelgrave. You people always want to fuck your servants.

(DARCY raises her arm to hit him but he stops her.)

BUNCE: You haven't an idea in hell who I am.

DARCY: You're a sailor. You steal. You kill.

(BUNCE begins to run his hands along her arms, much as MORSE did earlier, slowly, watching her face to see what she can feel.)

BUNCE: I worked the Royal Navy off and on for eleven years. Here?

DARCY: No.

BUNCE: Deserted when I could. In between I skulked the city. There?

(DARCY shakes her head 'no.' BUNCE moves on slowly to touch her shoulders and neck.)

BUNCE: I got picked up on the waters—here—?

DARCY: Yes.

BUNCE: —by the Spaniards and served them against the French. There?

(DARCY *shakes her head 'no'.*)

BUNCE: Then the Hollanders against the English.

(BUNCE *goes down on his knees. He puts his hands under her dress to touch her ankles. We cannot see his hands or her legs as her dress is long. She doesn't stop him, though she looks to see if* SNELGRAVE *is still sleeping. The rest of the scene should be very subtle.* DARCY *does her best to hide both her fear and pleasure and she hides them very well. Now and again she repeats his words.*)

BUNCE: Then I was taken up again by the English out of Dunkirker and served against the Hollanders. *(Beat)* There?

(Moving his hands higher up her legs)

BUNCE: There?

DARCY: I don't know. Yes. I think so.

BUNCE: Last I was taken by the Turks—

DARCY: The Turks.

BUNCE: Where I was forced to serve them against the English, French, Dutch, and Spaniards and all Christendom. The last time I got picked up, I was in Church.

DARCY: Church.

BUNCE: In Bristol. The press gangs had orders to pick up all men without property, above fifteen. They must have raided half a dozen churches to get the men they needed.

(Moving his hands up further)

BUNCE: And here? *(Beat)* Most of those lads didn't know the first thing about sailing, let alone war. In the first hours we sailed, two of them got tangled in the mizzen shrouds and swept overboard. Another fell from the jib boom.

DARCY: Jib boom?

BUNCE: There was one boy who took sick with the motion. His neck and face swelled with the retching. Then his tongue went black. He held out his arms to us. For mercy. Then he vomited his stomach up into his hands and died.

(Touching her)

BUNCE: This? Yeah. Here. *(Beat)* We sailed to battle the Dutch at Tescell.

DARCY: Tescell.

BUNCE: Over twenty ships went down on fire. And the gulls. Screaming above the cannons. They wouldn't fly from the ships. Here? *(Beat)* Some of them. Their wings caught fire, so close did they circle the sinking masts. When the battle was over, half of the men. Dead in the water. Floating face down in the waves, still in the Sunday suits they'd been picked up in. *(Beat)* I sailed ships for navies most of my life.

(Touching her intimately)

BUNCE: And here? Yeah. Right here. *(Beat)* In all that time I didn't kill. *(Beat)* Mrs Snelgrave?

DARCY: *(Whispers)* Yes.

BUNCE: I never killed. It was in me though. Do you want me to stop?

(DARCY does not answer him.)

(End Scene Three)

Scene Four

(SNELGRAVE still tied in his chair. BUNCE curled up and asleep on his mat. He doesn't stir through the entire scene. MORSE sits and plays with two small cloth-and-stick dolls. She is wearing one of DARCY's dresses, which doesn't fit her at all, but she is happy to be dressed in it.)

MORSE: And the two lovers were happy and the sky a
blue grape and the birds sang. *(To* SNELGRAVE*)* Can you
make the tweet of the birds?

SNELGRAVE: If you untie me.

MORSE: *(Uses the doll to speak)* I can't, Mr Snelgrave.
If I let you go, you will break me in half with your cane.
(Beat) If you don't want to play, then shut up. *(Beat)*
And the two lovers were happy and the sky a fat apple
and the birds sang. And the world—

*(*SNELGRAVE *begins to make bird sounds.* MORSE *listens a
moment. She approves.)*

MORSE: And the birds sang sweetly and the world was
good and—

(She looks at SNELGRAVE*'s bare feet.)*

MORSE: —even the rich had shoes. But one day the
world changed. *(She strikes a tinderbox.)* And it never
changed back. *(She holds one of the dolls near the flame.)*

SNELGRAVE: Don't do that. *(Beat)* Please.

MORSE: The young man said. But the fire angel would
have her heart.

*(She lights the stick doll on fire and sets it on the floor to
burn. They watch it burn out.)*

MORSE: Even her voice was burned, but still he heard
her say, "Hold me", and the young man came to her
and—

SNELGRAVE: No. He didn't come to her. He was a
coward, your man.

*(*DARCY *almost enters the room but then stops and watches
them. They are intent on the story and do not see her.)*

MORSE: He knelt down beside her—

SNELGRAVE: He walked away.

MORSE: —and put his hand into the ashes that were her
body.

SNELGRAVE: He turned his back.

MORSE: The young man sifted the ashes until he found what was left of her heart.

SNELGRAVE: Small and black and empty it was—

MORSE: But it was her heart.

SNELGRAVE: And the young man put the burnt organ—

MORSE: No bigger than a walnut shell—

SNELGRAVE: —into a glass of his own blood.

(While MORSE *speaks the following,* SNELGRAVE *again whistles softly as before.)*

MORSE: And there the heart drank and drank until it was plump once more. And though the prince could never hold her in his arms again, she being now only the size of his palm, he could caress her with his fingers and when it was winter the heart lay against his cold breast and kept him warm.

*(*DARCY *exits. They do not notice.)*

SNELGRAVE: I'm an ordinary man. I never meant to be cruel.

MORSE: Neither did Sir Braithwaite. And yet when my mother, a maid in his house for fourteen years, came to him one morning with the black tokens on her neck, he locked her in the root cellar. He was afraid they'd close up his house if they found out someone had taken sick. Neither food nor water he gave her. I lay outside the cellar door. With the door between us, we slept with our mouths to the crack so that we could feel each other's breath.

SNELGRAVE: We didn't lock up our maids. We called for a surgeon.

MORSE: She said, "Hold me", because she was cold, but the door was between us and I could not hold her.

SNELGRAVE: Enough of this. Get me some water, child.

MORSE: Did you bring them water when they were dying?

SNELGRAVE: Yes.

MORSE: You lie. You sent your boy to do it. You never looked on them once they were sick.

SNELGRAVE: I couldn't help them. It was God's wish.

MORSE: You locked them in the cellar.

SNELGRAVE: That's not true.

MORSE: And they died in the dirt and blood of their own bodies. And their last breath blew under the door and found your fat mouth and hid inside it and waited for the proper moment to fill your throat.

SNELGRAVE: You are an evil, evil girl. If your mother were alive—

MORSE: My mother lives in your mouth, and one day she will choke you.

SNELGRAVE: Who's your father, girl?

MORSE: I was born from a piece of broken star that pierced my mother's heart.

SNELGRAVE: More likely Sir Braithwaite. Masters make free with their maids. I'll be honest. I've done so myself. Perhaps this gentleman you despise and ridicule was your own father. Heh? How about that, little girl? Ever thought of that?

(MORSE *stands staring at him some moments. Then she quickly lifts the long dress and flashes him. This action is not seductive. For* MORSE *it is as though she were pissing on him. After a moment, he turns his head away. She picks up the doll that played the prince. The remains of the burnt doll on the floor she scatters with a kick.*)

(*End Scene Four*)

Scene Five

(DARCY, BUNCE, MORSE, *and* SNELGRAVE, *still tied to his chair.* MORSE *has taken off* DARCY'*s dress and goes about in her long johns again.* SNELGRAVE *is dressed in* BUNCE'*s clothes, which fit poorly.* BUNCE *is putting on* SNELGRAVE'*s pants. The shirt doesn't fit him so he throws it aside. There is laughter and an initial sense of merriment from all four of them.*)

SNELGRAVE: Ha! They're a poor fit. You see! Untie me, Darcy.

DARCY: Please stop asking me that. Tomorrow perhaps. Not today.

SNELGRAVE: Bunce. I'll pay you in gold if you let me go.

BUNCE: The child has already given me half your gold, sir.

SNELGRAVE: But I have more at the Navy Board. Much more.

MORSE: (*Brings the vinegar bucket and begins to wash* SNELGRAVE. *He pays no attention.*) First we clean the meat. Then we cook it.

SNELGRAVE: (*To* DARCY) You do realize we can't go on after this as man and wife.

DARCY: We haven't gone on as man and wife—

SNELGRAVE: I'll put you out in the streets.

DARCY: —since I was seventeen.

SNELGRAVE: You'll be the shame of the city. Less than a whore. You'll live in the kennel, stink—

DARCY: La, la. And I will strip and walk naked to your Navy Board, and in the courtyard I will dance.

MORSE: Like a pinecone on fire she'll dance.

SNELGRAVE: There's no life for you outside of this
marriage, outside of this house. Bunce can't take care
of you.

MORSE: But Bunce can tie knots. I can tie a catspaw best.
Mrs Snelgrave can do a flemish-eye faster than he can.

SNELGRAVE: Tying knots with Bunce now, are we?
How sweet. How delicious. Tell me, Bunce, what's
her cunny like?

(BUNCE *doesn't answer.*)

SNELGRAVE: Bread that's left too long in the oven?

DARCY: *(To* BUNCE*)* Why don't you answer him?

(*Silence some moments.* BUNCE *shrugs, then takes a drink of
water. He leans over* SNELGRAVE *as though to kiss him, and
almost kisses him but instead he lets the water trickle slowly
out of his mouth across* SNELGRAVE's *mouth and face.*
SNELGRAVE *is so shocked by the audacity and sensuality
of this act that by the time he resists,* BUNCE *is through.*)

BUNCE: That's your wife, sir. Though I haven't yet
had the pleasures you assume. Only with my left hand.
My right hand aches with jealousy.

(SNELGRAVE *closes his eyes and appears to be praying.*
BUNCE *looks at* DARCY *for approval. She blushes.*
SNELGRAVE *opens one eye and sees her blush. He spits at
her but misses.*)

SNELGRAVE: If all you needed was a man as low as this
to bring you round, I could have paid Kabe to do it.

MORSE: I saw Kabe's mousie once. Its tail was long and
skinny.

DARCY: No one brought me round, William. I've lain
beside you like a piece of old charcoal most of my life
and, well, if that's what I am—

SNELGRAVE: *(Interrupts)* I wouldn't expect much
pleasure in return, Bunce. She's an old woman.
Her mouth stinks. Her—

MORSE: *(Sticking her bare toe in his face)* What will you pay me if I let you suck my toe?

SNELGRAVE: You foul child!

DARCY: It seems centuries ago, but you used to weep at the pleasure I gave you.

MORSE: Kabe paid me a sugar-knot for a kiss.

SNELGRAVE: *(To* DARCY*)* You lie. *(To* BUNCE*)* I bet she hasn't pleased you, has she?

MORSE: Small fruits and berries for a suck on the little toes.

DARCY: Answer him, Bunce.

MORSE: Larger fruits for a suck on the big one.

BUNCE: No. She hasn't.

DARCY: *(To* SNELGRAVE*)* He's never asked me to.

SNELGRAVE: You think a man needs to ask?! *(To* BUNCE*)* Listen to that! She says you've never asked her!

BUNCE: Well, sir. I just sort of expected she'd take what she wanted. It's always been that way between us kind, hasn't it?

SNELGRAVE: Ha!

MORSE: Ha!

BUNCE: What's changed?

MORSE: You're wearing new shoes.

BUNCE: That I am. And a man in these shoes should be able to ask...

SNELGRAVE: Go on.

MORSE: Yes?

BUNCE: Will you, Mrs Snelgrave...

SNELGRAVE: Yes?

MORSE: Go on.

BUNCE: Bring. A poor sailor. And part-time servant. To his crisis?

(SNELGRAVE *bursts out laughing, and* MORSE *laughs too, copying* SNELGRAVE. BUNCE *blushes.*)

DARCY: I don't think I could—

SNELGRAVE: See? It wasn't only me. She didn't like it after the fire either.

DARCY: I don't know a great deal about—

SNELGRAVE: It was a horror even to lie beside her.

DARCY: Other people. Their bodies.

SNELGRAVE: For years, the smoke rose out of her mouth as she slept.

MORSE: But she could learn. Couldn't she, Mr Snelgrave?

SNELGRAVE: Learn? Her? Never, child.

MORSE: Of course she could. If Bunce stands here. And Mrs Snelgrave right there.

SNELGRAVE: What?

MORSE: Come on. Don't be stupid.

(*They follow her orders.*)

MORSE: Mrs Snelgrave puts her hands on his chest. Go on.

SNELGRAVE: His chest?

BUNCE: Isn't that my bit?

MORSE: Not this time, it isn't.

SNELGRAVE: You're all mad.

MORSE: Then she gives him a little kiss on the cheek.

(DARCY *does so.*)

SNELGRAVE: Mad!

MORSE: Then she takes off her glove. Mrs Snelgrave?

(*She takes off her glove.*)

MORSE: And she lets it drop to the floor. Like a leaf. Ha.

(DARCY *lets the glove drop.*)

MORSE: Then Mrs Snelgrave, she lets her hand slowly
move down his chest, slowly, down. Yes. To there.

(DARCY's *hand rests on* BUNCE's *belt.*)

SNELGRAVE: *(To* MORSE*)* Where were you schooled, slut?

MORSE: Keyholes. *(Beat)* And now it's only polite to
make sure Bunce is still with her, so she says, "May I?"

(DARCY *doesn't speak.*)

SNELGRAVE: She can't say it! Ha.

MORSE: "Do you want me to touch you?" she says.

(BUNCE *doesn't answer.*)

SNELGRAVE: "Yes, I do," he says.

MORSE: And then we do this.

(*She blindfolds* SNELGRAVE.)

SNELGRAVE: Hey! Devil's spawn. Take that off.

MORSE: And I go to the kitchen.

SNELGRAVE: Take it off!

(MORSE *sighs, takes the rag from the bucket, and puts it in
his mouth. She exits.*)

DARCY: *(Wanting* SNELGRAVE *to hear them)* Shhh.
I don't want my husband to hear us.

BUNCE: We'll be as quiet as the dead.

(SNELGRAVE *screams through his stuffed rag.*)

(*End Scene Five*)

Scene Six

(*Early morning light.* SNELGRAVE *slumped in his chair.*
MORSE *enters in a nightdress that is* SNELGRAVE's *shirt
that* BUNCE *discarded in the previous scene.* MORSE
*approaches him, closer, closer until their faces are almost
touching.*)

MORSE: That wasn't a poor bird you did yesterday.
It was quite good, really.

(She touches him, then shakes him. He is dead.)

MORSE: Where did you go, Mr Snelgrave?

(She unbuttons his shirt and checks his chest and neck.)

MORSE: You haven't even got the tokens.

(She slowly begins to untie SNELGRAVE *as she speaks the
following.)*

MORSE: Sir Braithwaite's daughter had a bird. A green
and black bird. Whack, whack went her stick on my
back when I swept. Then she'd let me hold the bird so
I'd stop my crying. The bird had a song like a long, long
spoon, and we could sip at it like jam. And the song put
a butterfly inside our mouths, and it opened its wings
in there and made us laugh. *(She sits with the rope in her
lap.)* But everyone died in that house. And then Lissa
was dying too, and we were alone, and she lay on the
floor with the tokens shining black on her neck. The
tokens would not break and run, and Lissa wept from
the pain. She said, "Hold me". *(Beat)* She could no
longer see and was blind. *(Beat)* She said, "Hold me",
and I said, "Give me your dress." She couldn't take it
off, because she was too weak, so I undressed her. Lissa
said, "Hold me now." She was small and thin without
her dress. I said, "Give me your shoes", and she let me
have them. I put on the dress and the shoes. I went to
the looking glass. The silk of the dress lapped at my
skin. The ruffles whispered hush, hush as I walked.
Lissa said, "Hold me, Morse. I'm so cold." I went to her
then. *(Beat)* But then she was. Dead. I sat beside her,
holding the bird. It sang for her. It sang for hours and
hours until its heart stopped in my hands. *(Beat)* It was
Lissa's bird. I could take her dress and shoes but I
couldn't take the bird. Even dead, it was Lissa's bird.
Not mine. *(Beat)* I opened her mouth and put the bird
inside.

(MORSE goes to SNELGRAVE.)

MORSE: You are dead. I can hold you.

(She gently embraces his body.)

(End Scene Six)

Scene Seven

(Below the window, outside, KABE is singing.)

KABE: Tyburn tree, Tyburn tree
Hang anybody but the poor man and me.

(BUNCE appears.)

BUNCE: Pssst.

KABE: Hang the King, Hang the Duke
If I survive you'll be the death of me.

BUNCE: I got gold.

KABE: Says the man in chains.

BUNCE: I'm going out through the cellar.

KABE: *(Ignoring BUNCE)* The King's coming back.

BUNCE: I got gold to pay you.

KABE: Kabe and King don't see eye to eye. Hell'll break loose. No place for a man of ability.

BUNCE: I'll throw in a pair of shoes the likes you've not seen before. Gentlemen's leather.

KABE: Chaos. Destruction. Mammon's back. Swarms, Sodom and all. Maybe I'll off to Oxford. Pass the monster on the way. Bow and wave.

BUNCE: And a pair of earrings.

KABE: Living's a nasty business.

BUNCE: I think they're emerald.

KABE: How's Mr Snelgrave this morning?

BUNCE: I'm not Snelgrave.

KABE: Yes, you are. *(Beat)* The gold and the silk suit.
Put the earrings in the pocket. You keep the shoes.
Dumb Samuel will be on some night this week. I can't
tell you when. Keep watch. He can't shout, but be
quick. They'll kill you.

BUNCE: *(About to thank him)* Kabe—

KABE: *(Interrupts)* I don't care enough about you to hate
you, Rabble. *(Beat)* Tell the girl she'll have to give me a
suck, on the mouth this time, or no deal. Said the cock
to the chicken.

BUNCE: I heard you.

KABE: *(Recites)* I don't like sailors. They stink of tar.
But my lass she smells of the falling star.

(BUNCE disappears from the window.)

KABE: *(Sings)*
Tyburn tree, Tyburn tree
Can't find work for any fee
The Plague's got your tongue, worm's at your bone
You're as near to me as the West Indy.

Tyburn tree, Tyburn tree.
Won't you, won't you make love to me!

(End Scene Seven)

Scene Eight

*(BUNCE is putting a few spare items, a shirt, bread, onto a
piece of cloth that he'll tie up as a sack. MORSE watches him.
SNELGRAVE sits dead in his chair, a small cloth over his face.)*

BUNCE: Don't know. Out of the city if I can. And find
work. Back up North maybe. Some quiet parish that's
not got too many poor. God willing.

MORSE: You don't believe in God.

BUNCE: If there's employment, I'll believe and more.

MORSE: You could stay.

BUNCE: Not now. I'd might as well rope myself and walk to Tyburn. Save them and me trouble.

MORSE: But my word and Mrs Snelgrave's...

BUNCE: Her word? Can't trust that the right story would stick in her mouth. Who's to say she wouldn't be front row just to see me rise up in me britches after I drop down and into hell.

MORSE: Rise up in your britches?

BUNCE: It's the rush of blood to your, to me... I can't stay.

MORSE: (Nodding towards SNELGRAVE) They have to come and get him. (Beat) They'll throw him in the pits, though it wasn't plague, won't they?

BUNCE: He won't care.

MORSE: I don't mind him here. Now. He doesn't smell.

BUNCE: Not yet.

MORSE: And me?

BUNCE: Mrs Snelgrave will care for you.

MORSE: She has no heart. That's what she told me.

BUNCE: Trust her; she's a liar.

MORSE: You didn't mind how she felt? Her skin.

BUNCE: You don't feel with your hands.

MORSE: (Holding out her arms) Am I soft?

BUNCE: (Touches her arm) You are. (Beat) You feel. Alive.

MORSE: Everyone leaves.

BUNCE: Ay.

MORSE: Even when they stay.

(MORSE takes the stick doll she didn't burn out of her pocket and puts it on the small pile BUNCE is about to wrap up.)

MORSE: It wants to go with you.

BUNCE: (Picking up the stick doll and looking at it) Who is it?

MORSE: It's me.

(BUNCE *puts the stick doll on his pile and ties it all into a bundle. Then he takes some rope from his pocket to show* MORSE *one more knot.* DARCY *enters and stands watching them. They don't notice her.*)

BUNCE: I'll show you a last one, then I'm off. Thumb knot you use to tie the mouse and collar on the mast. You always go in here, not around. A good knot is like a dead man's heart; you can't break it.

(BUNCE *notices* DARCY *standing there. She is quietly watching them. Her face and hair are wet with sweat.*)

MORSE: *(Making the knot)* You can't break my heart. It's made of water.

(She shows him her knot. Then she too sees DARCY.*)*

BUNCE: Your dress is wet.

DARCY: That's because my head is full. Of ocean. And the shells are sliding back and forth in my ears.

(Touching her head)

DARCY: It's hot in here. Very hot.

BUNCE: *(To* MORSE*)* Get a blanket.

(MORSE *stands transfixed on* DARCY.*)*

BUNCE: A blanket! And some towels.

(MORSE *gets them.*)

DARCY: You mustn't bother.

(BUNCE *nears her.*)

DARCY: Stay back.

BUNCE: The tokens. Are they on your neck or thighs?

DARCY: They're in my mind.

BUNCE: We've got to make a fire. Are the botches hard yet?

(DARCY *doesn't answer. He approaches her again.*)

BUNCE: Take off your dress. Let me look.

DARCY: Never. *(Beat)* You must get out. Take the child with you. *(She reveals a knife.)* I will not hesitate.

BUNCE: *(He moves close enough to her so she can cut him.)* Neither will I.

(She lowers the knife. Weakened by fever, she sits. BUNCE drops to his knees and raises her skirts.)

BUNCE: *(To MORSE)* It's her thighs. Get some coals from the kitchen. And some wet cloth.

(MORSE exits. BUNCE puts his arms under her dress and begins to massage her thighs vigorously.)

BUNCE: We've got to soften the botches. With heat. Then we can lance them.

(DARCY sits in a daze. She stares at SNELGRAVE in his chair.)

DARCY: Take it off.

(BUNCE starts to unbutton her dress. She stops him.)

DARCY: The cloth.

(DARCY indicates SNELGRAVE. BUNCE removes the small cloth that was covering SNELGRAVE's face. MORSE returns with a bucket of coals and wet clothes.)

DARCY: Is he laughing, Morse?

(MORSE looks at SNELGRAVE's face.)

MORSE: No, Mrs Snelgrave. He's weeping. But he's so far away we can't hear him.

DARCY: Is he cold?

(MORSE touches SNELGRAVE's arm. BUNCE rips up cloth.)

MORSE: Like snow, he is.

DARCY: I envy him.

MORSE: Does it hurt?

DARCY: Here.

(Indicating her stomach)

DARCY: As though I had swallowed. Large pieces of glass.

(BUNCE *takes up a hot coal and wraps it in the wet cloth.*)

BUNCE: You'll feel this, Mrs Snelgrave.

(*He puts them under* DARCY's *dress, against her skin.* DARCY *flinches strongly at the heat.*)

MORSE: (*Attempting to distract her*) Did you care for him?

DARCY: Who?

MORSE: Mr Snelgrave.

DARCY: I knew him only as a boy. After the fire, he bore the same name, but that was the only resemblance. Yes. As a boy. Perhaps I loved him. Look at him there. Can you believe it, Morse? We used to touch each other for hours. We thought we were remaking ourselves. Perhaps we were. For each morning we were someone new and the world was almost a surprise, like biting into a piece of fruit with your eyes closed. (*Beat*) No more, Bunce. Please. It does no good.

(BUNCE *puts another wrapped piece of coal under her dress.* DARCY *stifles a scream.*)

MORSE: (*Distracting* DARCY) Did William kiss you many, many times, Mrs Snelgrave?

DARCY: Many, many times. And his tongue so cold. It covered my skin with frost.

(DARCY *screams again.* BUNCE *takes the knife from her hand and begins to bring it under her skirt to lance the tokens. Suddenly* DARCY *is completely lucid. She stops* BUNCE's *hand.*)

DARCY: No.

BUNCE: If I can make them run there's a chance.

DARCY: God damn you, Bunce. The life is pouring out of me. (*Shouts*) Help me! (*Quietly*) Help me.

BUNCE: I'm trying to save your life.

DARCY: That's not what I mean.

(BUNCE *shakes his head 'no'*. MORSE *moves away and watches them.*)

DARCY: Do you love me?

(*For a moment,* BUNCE *laughs in a desperate manner.*)

DARCY: I said, "Do you love me?"

BUNCE: Not enough to kill you.

DARCY: Then. Let me.

BUNCE: Don't ask. Shhh. Please.

(BUNCE *lays his head in her lap. She takes the knife from his hand.*)

BUNCE: I haven't the courage.

(*There is silence for some moments.*)

MORSE: I do.

DARCY: You're not afraid?

(MORSE *nods 'no'.*)

DARCY: Take my hand. Come then. Now squeeze it with all your might.

(MORSE *does so.*)

MORSE: I'm strong. I am.

BUNCE: No.

DARCY: If you stop me, you'll regret it. And I'll curse you the moment I die. (*Beat*) You can leave the room, sailor. I'm not asking you to stay.

(BUNCE *stares at her for what seems a long time. Then he kisses her, gently, on the forehead. As he begins to move away, she pulls him back and forces him to kiss her, hard, on the mouth. Then* BUNCE *goes to his mat and kneels there, his face to the wall.* DARCY *speaks to* MORSE.)

DARCY: So you will help me.

MORSE: What will you give me?

DARCY: Well, I don't think I have anything left.

MORSE: Your gloves.

DARCY: Alright, my gloves.

(DARCY *removes her gloves. She puts* MORSE's *hands on the knife and her own hands over* MORSE's.)

DARCY: You must not waver, Morse. Not for one moment. Do you understand?

(MORSE *nods.* DARCY *places the blade point against her chest, over her heart.* DARCY *closes her eyes.*)

MORSE: Don't close your eyes, Mrs Snelgrave. All you'll see is blackness.

(MORSE *puts her face close to* DARCY's *face.*)

MORSE: Look at me. At my face.

(DARCY *opens her eyes.*)

DARCY: Yes.

MORSE: The breath of a child has passed through the lungs of an angel. You said that.

(DARCY *nods.*)

MORSE: So the breath of an angel now covers your face. Can you feel it?

(*She blows on* DARCY's *face.*)

MORSE: And I will hold you, hush, hush. The angel's tongue is plump with blood and my mouth so cold it covers your skin with snow as the flames, like scissors, open your dress. And my kiss is a leaf. It falls from the sky and comes to rest on your breast. And my kiss is strong and pierces your heart—

(MORSE *helps* DARCY *drive the knife into* DARCY's *heart.*)

MORSE: Like a secret from God.

(MORSE *pulls out the knife.* DARCY *is dead.* MORSE *holds the knife out to* BUNCE. MORSE *is completely still, perhaps in shock. Finally* BUNCE *turns around.*)

MORSE: It is done. We are dead.

(*End Scene Eight*)

Scene Nine

(Music of a funeral procession, Gregorian chants. Darkness.
In the cell or place of confinement as in previous scenes.
In the shadows we see the dead SNELGRAVES, *still in their*
chairs. Nothing of BUNCE *or of* BUNCE's *presence remains.*
MORSE *stands center stage, again in her dirty dress.)*

MORSE: Can I go now? *(Beat)* There's nothing more to
tell of them.

Years it was. Or weeks and days, by the time the doors
were opened. The city was empty. The air was sweet
with sugar and piss. And it was quiet. So quiet. And
I walked down to the quay side. The boats were still.
There was no wind. The river was not moving.
Everyone had gone. One way or another.

*(*KABE *enters in the shadows. He covers* SNELGRAVE *with a*
cloth.)

MORSE: I stood by the banks and looked in the water.
There were no fish. There was nothing but water. Water
that didn't move. But then, I saw a child floating there.
On her back. She rose so close to the surface I could
have touched her. A girl of nine or ten. Pale and blond
she was. And naked. She had no marks. In each hand
she clutched a fist of black hair. Her mouth was open
and filled with the river. As I reached in the water to
touch her, a ship hoisted its sail. A door slammed in the
street. One, two, three voices called out to one other.
A bell rang. And the city came alive once more. *(Sings)*
Oranges and lemons
Sing the bells of St Clements.

*(*KABE *covers* DARCY *with a cloth.)*

MORSE: When I looked down in the water again for the
body of the child, it was gone. And I was glad. I was
glad it had gone.

(KABE *exits.*)

MORSE: Kabe once said to me, "Our lives are just a splash of water on a stone. Nothing more." *(She kneels, as though in prayer.)* Then I am the stone on which they fell. And they have marked me.

So beware.

Because I loved them, and they have marked me.

(MORSE sits and takes the orange from her pocket. She holds the orange in her lap, looking at it, her head bowed. We hear KABE singing, offstage, though his voice fills the entire cell.)

KABE: Farewell said the scab to the itch
Farewell said the crab to its crotch
Farewell said the plague to death's ditch
Farewell said the dead to their watch.

(MORSE tosses the orange high into the air. Just as she catches it, the lights go black.)

END OF PLAY

BROADWAY PLAY PUBLISHING INC

TOP TEN BEST SELLING
FULL-LENGTH PLAYS AND
FULL-LENGTH PLAY COLLECTIONS

AVEN'U BOYS

THE BROTHERS KARAMAZOV

THE IMMIGRANT

ONE FLEA SPARE

ON THE VERGE

PLAYS BY TONY KUSHNER
(CONTAINING A BRIGHT ROOM CALLED DAY,
THE ILLUSION, & SLAVS!)

PLAYS BY AISHAH RAHMAN
(CONTAINING THE MOJO AND THE SAYSO,
UNFINISHED WOMEN...,
& ONLY IN AMERICA)

PRELUDE TO A KISS

TALES OF THE LOST FORMICANS

TO GILLIAN ON HER 37TH BIRTHDAY